Arran

The Glens & the Brave

Mackenzie MacBride

Alpha Editions

This edition published in 2019

ISBN : 9789353709280

Design and Setting By
Alpha Editions
email - alphaedis@gmail.com

This book is a reproduction of an important historical work. Alpha Editions uses the best technology to reproduce historical work in the same manner it was first published to preserve its original nature. Any marks or number seen are left intentionally to preserve its true form.

ARRAN OF THE BENS
THE GLENS & THE BRAVE

BY MACKENZIE MACBRIDE, F.S.A.(SCOT.)

WITH ILLUSTRATIONS IN COLOUR BY

J. LAWTON WINGATE, R.S.A.

CHICAGO
A. C. McCLURG & CO.
EDINBURGH: T. N. FOULIS
1911

Printed in Great Britain

CONTENTS

PART I

THE CHARM OF ARRAN

CHAP.   PAGE
- I. THE CHARM OF ARRAN 3
- II. THE LAND BETWEEN SKY AND WATER . 8
   THE HOLY ISLAND
- III. ARRAN'S ROMANCES 12
   KING ROBERT BRUCE — CROMWELL AND ARRAN

PART II

HISTORICAL REMAINS

- IV. ARRAN'S ANCIENT CHAPELS . . . 21
   KILBRIDE — KILMORY — SHISKEN CHAPEL — SANNOX CHAPEL — GLEN ASHDALE CHAPEL
- V. ARRAN'S CASTLES 27
   BRODICK CASTLE — LOCHRANZA CASTLE — THE GEOLOGY OF ARRAN

CONTENTS

CHAP.   PAGE

VI. THE CAVES OF ARRAN 31
      FINGAL'S CAVE — THE PREACHING CAVE AT KILPATRICK — THE WONDROUS BAUL OF SAINT MULUY

PART III

ARRAN IN THE EIGHTEENTH CENTURY

VII. ARRAN IN THE EIGHTEENTH CENTURY . 40
      THE OLD RUNRIG SYSTEM — JOHN BURRELL — HIS SCHEME OF IMPROVEMENT — THE GREAT REVOLUTION — SMUGGLING IN ARRAN — FAMOUS ARRAN PREACHERS — THE ARRAN EVICTIONS — WHAT PENNANT SAW — ARRAN AND THE FORTY-FIVE

PART IV

THE BRANDANI

VIII. OLD FAMILIES IN ARRAN . . . 69
      THE ARRAN AND BUTE BARONS

IX. THE BRANDANES 76
      OR, MEN OF ARRAN AND BUTE

X. THE LANGUAGE OF ARRAN . . . 81
      THE AUTHOR OF THE FIRST GAELIC DICTIONARY : WILLIAM SHAW — DANIEL MACMILLAN

CONTENTS

PART V

OUR EARLY ANCESTORS IN ARRAN

CHAP.		PAGE
XI.	Arran's Wealth of Prehistoric Remains	91
	THE ETHNOLOGY OF ARRAN	
XII.	Ancient Forts and Camps	103
	DRUMADOON—TOR CAISTEAL—GLEN ASHDALE—KING'S CROSS—DUN FION—CRAIG NA CUIROCH—TORNANSCHIAN	

PART VI

ARRAN—THE BATTLE-GROUND OF THE VIKING AGE

XIII.	Arran in the Viking Age	113
	THE CHRISTIANS OF IONA—THE VALE OF SHISKEN AND MACHRIE MOOR	
XIV.	The Arran Men at the Battle of Brunanburh	126
	THE FLEET IN LAMLASH BAY—MAGNUS BAREFOOT	
XV.	Somerled, the Hammer of the Norsemen	136
XVI.	How King Hakon Fought at Largs	145
XVII.	King Hakon at Lamlash	154

PART VII

THE DAYS OF WALLACE

XVIII.	The Great War of Independence	159
	THE BATTLE OF STIRLING BRIDGE—THE BRANDANES AT THE BATTLE OF FALKIRK—HOW THE BRANDANES COVERED THE RETREAT—THE BRANDANES AT PERTH—EDWARD'S VENGEANCE	

CONTENTS

PART VIII

HOW THE ARRAN MEN SHELTERED KING ROBERT BRUCE

CHAP. PAGE
XIX. THE AMBUSH AT BRODICK CASTLE . . 189
BRUCE AND THE SPIDER—THE RED LIGHT ON TURNBERRY BEACON—THE BRANDANES AT BANNOCKBURN

PART IX

WHAT THE BRANDANES DID FOR THE STEWARTS

XX. WHAT THE BRANDANES DID FOR THE STEWARTS 207
THE BATTLE OF THE STONES—THE STEWARD'S ESCAPE FROM ROTHESAY CASTLE—THE KING'S BODYGUARD—THE BATTLES OF WILLIAM THE LYON AND THE DISASTER AT PINKIE

PART X

THE LATER LORDS OF ARRAN

XXI. THE LATER LORDS OF ARRAN . 221
THE BOYDS—THE HAMILTONS—"LADY MARY"

ILLUSTRATIONS
Reproduced from Oil Paintings by
J. LAWTON WINGATE, R.S.A.

GOATFELL FROM THE ROAD BETWEEN LAMLASH AND BRODICK . . .	*Frontispiece*
SUNSET AT MOUTH OF THE MACHRIE .	*Page* 8
AILSA CRAIG AND PLADDA LIGHTHOUSE FROM KILDONAN	,, 16
LOCHRANZA AND CASTLE . . .	,, 24
OLD BRIDGE: NORTH GLEN SANNOX .	,, 40
CORN CUTTING	,, 56
OLD ARRAN HOUSES, WHITING BAY .	,, 72
HARVESTING—TORMORE . . .	,, 88
CAISTEAL ABHAIL	,, 104
THE EDGE OF THE SHISKEN MOOR .	,, 120
DRUMADOON BAY	,, 136
THE OLD PIER, LAMLASH, AND THE HOLY ISLAND	,, 152
CLOUDS MOVING OVER A MOOR: BEN ARDVEN IN DISTANCE . . .	,, 168
GREY CLOUDLAND: SOUND OF KILBRANNAN	,, 184
WHITING BAY FROM THE KILDONAN ROAD	,, 200
THE APPROACH OF NIGHT—OVER THE SOUND OF KILBRANNAN . . .	,, 216

ARRAN

" HERE, as of old, the dreaming hours fulfil
  Their ancient pledge, and flower in sunlit days
  Above thy pastoral slopes and wave-washed bays
Where melody and colour merge and thrill.
Thy chosen Priestess, Beauty, beckons still
From whin-clad straths and heather-haunted ways,
  Or lies in wait along the scented braes,
  Or chains a leafy thought from hill to hill.

Bruce found a shelter, lovely Isle, in thee
When o'er his head the cloud of menace rolled,
He saw thy rock-strewn mountains tipped with gold
When morning mounted sovran from the sea,
  And on thy bosom, fold on misty fold,
  Beheld her dew-stained garments floating free."

FERDINAND E. KAPPEY.

PART I
THE CHARM OF ARRAN

CHAPTER I

THE CHARM OF ARRAN

BOTH the stranger and the native find something peculiarly alluring in Arran; and, though it is but a small island of twenty odd miles by seven, and the world is a large place, few who have known it fail to keep it amongst their cherished remembrances. I know an artist who has visited it regularly for forty years, and who starts again this autumn with a full programme of work already mapped out, and he would be the first to admit that much of his best work he owes to the pastoral loveliness and fine atmospheric effects so notable in the south of Arran. There are many, too, who, after thirty or forty years spent in the busiest cities, have been glad to turn their steps to their native island; others there are who, in the full tide of manhood, have forsaken the excitements of America and Australia and come home to settle in the smallest of villages close by Kilbrannan Sound. Paterson, a Lowlander, writing in 1834, says: "That the Highlanders of Scotland feel the love of country very strongly is unquestionable; and that it has a beneficial effect on their moral conduct is as certain. The dread of being expelled from Arran has more efficacy in restraining those of its inhabitants who may be inclined to dishonest, vicious, or idle courses, than all the penal laws in force."

What, then, is it that Arran holds that is so great an attraction? It is probably no one thing: the wonderful beauty of the Brodick lanes, with their views of Goatfell's great peak varied in character daily, nay sometimes hourly, but always lovely and commanding; the sweet scent of the surrounding woods, fir and birch, myrtle and heath, and of the hundred and one wild flowers of Arran, all lend their subtle contributions. But, indeed, the whole of the great groups of hills which stretch across the centre of the island, ranging in height from the 2866 feet of Goatfell to 600 or 800 feet in the southern district, have qualities which are rare. It would be difficult to find in a small space, even in Skye of the Mists or Mull of the Bens, mountains as weird, black, titanic as the Devil's Punch Bowl or Cioch nan h'oige (the Maiden's Breast), which alters so swiftly, mystically; now almost invisible, merged in the surrounding peaks, now a mere cone leaning obliquely southward; while now, seen from Sannox moor, it stands up threateningly, overwhelmingly, right above you. Nor in all the hills of the west can there be found anything so like an enchanted fortress of the Arabian Nights as the wonderful Caisteal Abhail (Casteel Aval), crowning its huge granite crag over sheer black precipices nearly three thousand feet below. And this is not all, for the great hill at the back, Ceum na Cailleach, is formed in the same cyclopean spirit, and its fantastic pinnacles seem to tell of further battlements beyond for those to climb who would attempt the strongholds of the gods. And there again, to the left of wonderful Sannox glen, stands Cir Mhor, aloft, aloof, filling up in solitary grandeur the space between Caisteal Abhail and Cioch nan h'oige. Where can we see anything as strange and fantastical as this group approached from Sannox glen?

But, of course, it may be seen from many parts of the island, nay, it is difficult to lose, it is everywhere, much as the Paps of Jura Island are visible over half the Kintyre coast, or the Goatfell group are everywhere with us when we journey in southern Arran or on the coast of Ayr and Renfrew. Mr. Lawton Wingate gives us a charming distant view of this range, for instance, from Largybeg; and a mountain climber, Mr. Stewart Orr, has sat lovingly close to the heart of the hills through dark nights in order to give us his pictures of their more intimate and undiscovered moods when flushed with the rosy colours of the dawn.

Certainly much of the charm of Arran arises from the presence of this stately concourse; but they are not all the hills the island boasts. Am Bhinnean in the same neighbourhood has many moods, and looks down upon us, from above the white cottages and stretch of wood on the Corrie shore, with all the dignity and splendour of a Sultan.

The Cuchullin range in Skye, though it has the upright peaks, lacks the grand horizontal lines like that of Suidhe-Feargus, which at Sannox are so finely symmetrical, and group so superbly round that solemn and inspiring spot.

The next view in point of grandeur is perhaps that of Goatfell towering up over the woods of Brodick Castle, seen from the cross roads, and along the Corrie shore as far as Ard na Beithe (point of the birch trees). The view, especially on a grey and sultry day, so subtly Oriental in suggestion, so wide, so dominated by the bare outline of the great cone rising out of the beech woods and pastures, cannot be equalled in the West Highlands for its power of capturing the senses, save perhaps in the approach to Benmore from the Holy Loch in Cowal, or the view of the Paps of Glencoe from Ballachulish.

CHAPTER II

THE LAND BETWEEN SKY AND WATER

Merrily rocks the boat,
    The Bell-buoy tosses and twirls,
And the bubbles that shoreward float
    Are as full of colour as pearls.

All the hues of the prism they show—
    The glitter of crimson dyes,
The orange of sunset glow,
    And the purple of morning skies.

The sands are a silver sheet,
    And the waves a revel of light,
Where motion and music meet,
    And colour and form unite.

From the black cliff's perilous steeps,
    The grass in the gale swings free;
The sea in the sunlight leaps,
    And the great clouds dip to the sea.

DAVID GOW.

Who again has not, like Mr. David Gow, felt the spell of Arran's waters, sparkling and flashing with a million white crests, breaking

SUNSET AT MOUTH OF THE MACHRIE
From a painting by
J. LAWTON WINGATE, R.S.A.

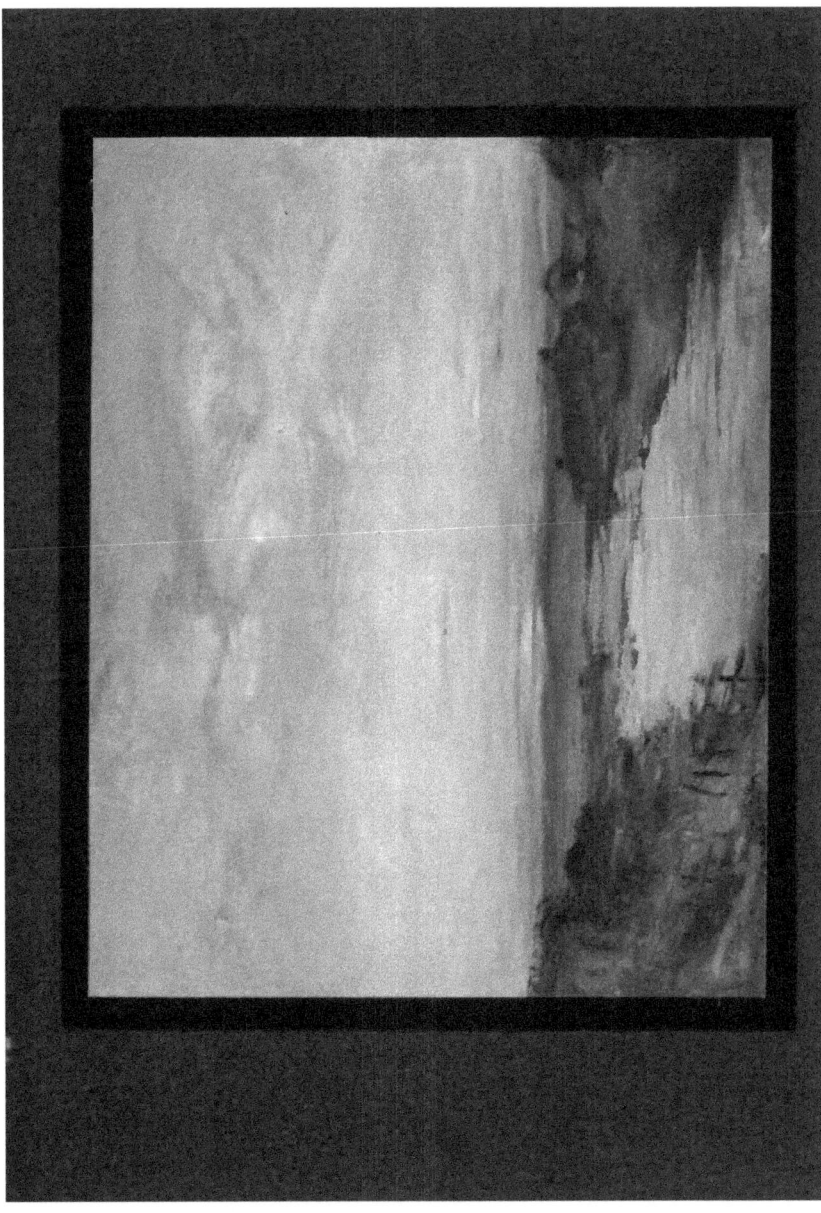

sharp and clear as crystals on rock and shingle, or rolling creamily like liquid amber on some smooth stretch of pink-white sand. Its seas, too, have a thousand shades of green, from fairest olive to deepest emerald; its burns a thousand tones of brown, from that of a dark cairngorm stone to the yellow of a cornelian. And just so the mists and distances vary in shades of grey and blue as delicate as that of the mantle of Queen Maev herself, famous in Keltic story. The passing shower or the passing cloud coming down from the narrow seas to northward, or up over Pladda and Ailsa Craig; or the storm-wind from the Atlantic that breaks on the shores of her old kinsman in legend and in blood, Kintyre; all these reflect jewellery of rare colours upon Arran seas and burns and hills. Lying prone between sky and water, it vibrates and reflects like a sensitive maid all the moods of nature —smiles, storms, tears. Certainly if it is monotony that kills, then one should live longest in Arran, changeful as sweet seventeen herself, least monotonous of lands. There Nature's hand never stays, is never idle. Compare it to an Italian coast, where she dawdles and languishes under a sky of perpetual blue and a blazing sun. East is not more remote from west, or north from south, or the gorgeous wardrobe of the Queen of Sheba from that of a London scullery-maid.

THE HOLY ISLAND

Another of Arran's charms is certainly cast by the Holy Island in the famous bay of Lamlash. There gathered the fleet that fought the Saxon King Athelstan at the great battle of Brunanburh, made famous in the finest of early English poems; there too, many centuries later, came Hakon of Norway with his ships, which, tempest aided, the Scottish king defeated utterly. Thus Arran was made the scene of the last act in the Norse incursions on the western coast, as it not improbably had been of the first, for it must have tempted all comers by its exposed position and the wealth of the industrious plain of Shisken and Machrie. To the Holy Island came also St. Molios, who lived in the cave associated with his name, on the walls of which have been deciphered some runic characters. These were once held to refer to Nicolas, a priest of Argyll; but a writer in *The Book of Arran* now states that they refer to a prosaically named Norseman, possibly a mere trader, one Uilaeikr Stallr; much as the white stone which was discovered by Mr. Pickwick was proved to bear the words "Bill Stumps, his mark." The island, like in shape to a lion couchant, forms a most picturesque outpost to the southern end of the great bay of Brodick.

CHAPTER III

ARRAN'S ROMANCES

MANY races have left their mark on Arran, have spilt their blood to hold it, have left their romances behind upon its hill-tops and its shores to redeem it from the commercialism of our time. The men of the Stone Age, of the Bronze period, the early Keltic period, did each some little to emancipate it from barbarism, till the splendid Dalriadic colonists came and finally broke its chains, making it partaker for a time of the noblest civilisation the world has yet known. But alas! its very wealth brought the Norse sea-rover who destroyed all, all but the fighting, clannish instinct of the "Kelt" which was to overcome the Northman in the end, so that not one fragment of all his conquests should remain to him. Of course, it is always more easy to destroy than to create, and so a rough hammer may shatter the Portland vase, a rough sword the monastery of Iona, and all the promise of good that lay in Dalriada.

Arran was at that time no wilderness; it was only six miles distant from the capital of a race who had been Christians for some 500 years, and whose blood it undoubtedly shared: a race who were skilled in the arts as their forbears in Ireland had been for centuries, and possessed some of the learning and the refinement which had made Ireland famous, and attracted to her shores scholars from every nation. The immense difference between them and the Norse intruders is curiously illustrated in the following passage from Mr. Henderson's *Norse Influence on Celtic Scotland*—"The kindly temperament of King Brian of Munster, heightened by his belief probably, was noticeable to the Saga writer, and I may adduce it as a parallel to the softening influence which contact with the West men sooner or later produced in the fierce followers of Odin. 'He (Brian),' says the Saga, 'was the best-natured of all kings;

thrice would he forgive all outlaws the same offence before he had them tried by the law, and from this it will be seen what a king he must have been.'"

KING ROBERT BRUCE

Arran is also famous as the place where Robert Bruce sought shelter when in hiding from the soldiers of Edward of England. Tradition has it that to avoid his pursuers he moved about the island, sheltering at one time in the famous King's Cave at Drumadoon, and at another at the ancient prehistoric fort in beautiful Glen Cloy, called Tor na' shian, or Mound of the Fairies, from which a view is obtained of the whole of the glen. There, too, it is said, when hunted by bloodhounds, he used to take exercise by wading up and down the Glen Cloy burn at High Glen Cloy, where it runs under the fine woods of Kilmichael, the home of the MacLouies or Fullartons.

Whether or not the name of Glenrickard, which lies above the grounds of Kilmichael, refers to the story of Bruce in Glen Cloy, I cannot say, but the name seems to have no connection with the word "Rickard," as the Ordnance Department seem to have supposed. The pronunciation of a friend, who has lived in the glen all his life of some sixty or more years, is "Glenreegart," a name derived probably from the Gaelic words *glen* and *righ* and *gart*, which give us the glen of the king's sanctuary or enclosure. The name may, of course, be of earlier origin than the time of Bruce, and might have been acquired from some legend invented to account for the great, twenty feet long, chambered cairn in which were buried our remote forbears, chiefs, and kings. It is now a children's plaything.

> "Imperious Cæsar, dead and turned to clay,
> Might stop a hole to keep the wind away."

The site of the original Kilmichael house was on the spot where Dr. Robertson-Fullarton has erected his observatory, and the ruins of Kilmichael Church were still visible a little to the north-east of this spot, close to the Glen Cloy burn, in Pennant's time.

Arran has also long been regarded as the

scene of the exploits of Fion (Fune) or Finn, and many place names tell of him and his followers, and of Ossian and Malvina. Indeed, many persons have held that the much disputed name, Arran, is from Ar Finn, the land of Finn, while others state that it is from Ar rinn, or land of the peaks; but the evidence seems insufficient to warrant a decided judgment in favour of either of these theories. It is clear that Fion and Ossian never had an existence in actual fact, but are of purely mythological origin, like the great Gaelic legend in which they figure; but so strong was the influence of the old mythology in the West at one time, and so saturated were the Arran people with the legends of the Feinne, that one is inclined to favour the definition of Ar Finn. The name of the hill Suidhe Feargus, in Glen Sannox, is that of Fion's son, and its beautiful outline is well worthy of the great romance linked with its name.

AILSA CRAIG AND PLADDA LIGHT-
HOUSE FROM KILDONAN
From a painting by
J. LAWTON WINGATE, R.S.A.

CROMWELL AND ARRAN

During the wars of Charles I. the Hamiltons stood for the King, but Brodick Castle was held at different times by both parties, and when the Earl of Stafford was about to reduce the West of Scotland to obedience, Argyll, with the Covenanters, took possession of Brodick. In 1644 the Marquis was created Duke of Hamilton for his services to Charles, but paid for his loyalty with his head when the Parliament finally overthrew the King. The Dutch ships were at that time hovering about the Outer Hebrides, and Cromwell's government had fear of them seizing the islands. They therefore garrisoned Brodick, and built the tower on the north-east side. The islanders, however, were enraged at the execution of their chief, and resented also the rough manners of the soldiery, who insulted their wives and daughters. They therefore set a trap for them when they were out foraging, and after chasing them along the Corrie shore, caught them at Sannox, and put them to the sword, the last being slain, according to tradition, at the "Killing Stone," on the Sannox shore. The next duke fought and died for Charles II. at Worcester, and with him were present the islanders, together with the other Highland clans.

PART II
HISTORICAL REMAINS

CHAPTER IV

ARRAN'S ANCIENT CHAPELS

MOST interesting of the old churches of Arran is the little chapel of St. Bride at Lamlash, where rest the remains of many generations of Arran people. In old times, possibly before the use of Kilbride graveyard, the burial-ground on the Holy Island was also popular as a burying-place.

KILBRIDE

In 1357 the churches of Kilbride and Kilmory were given by the lord of Arran, Sir John Menteith, to the monks of Kilmory, with their chapels. The charter of King David II., confirming the gift, is of some interest. It reads as follows—"To all the children of the blessed Mother Church now living, or yet to be born, who may see or hear these present writings, read:—John of Menteith, lord of Arran and of Knapdale. Health in the Lord for ever. Know that I for the good of my soul, and that of Katherine my late wife, and for the good of the souls of our ancestors and successors, have given, granted, and by this present charter of mine, confirmed to God and the blessed Virgin Mary, to good Wynnyn and to the monastery of Kylwynne in Conyngham, to the abbots and monks there worshipping God, and to those who will worship him there for ever, the right of presentation and patronage of the churches of St. Mary and St. Bride in the island of Arran, with their chapels, and with all other properties which to the said churches, with their chapels and lands, by right belong, to be held and possessed by the said monastery and monks for ever, with all rights belonging to them in fee-simple, and perpetual alms."

In 1452 James II. gave the crown lands of Kilbride and Kilmory, which yielded an annual rent of £56, 18s. 8d., to the Canons of Glasgow for a sum of eight hundred marks which had been lent by them to the King.

In 1540 the lands had again come into the possession of the crown, and Kilbride was then granted to Sir James Hamilton with the Earldom of Arran. Innes says the church stood originally on the north-west shore of Lamlash bay, on the spot marked in Blaeu's map "Marknaheglish." There are a few sculptured stones of interest in the graveyard, but many more have been destroyed. The most interesting and important was the ancient cross, which for many years lay on the family grave of the late Mr. John MacBride, who formerly farmed the Holy Island. On the removal of the stones from the burial-ground there he brought it to Kilbride. It has been recently removed to the front of the parish church at Lamlash. Stones of this type were often erected in graveyards where no church stood, to mark the sacred character of the place.

KILMORY

Innes and the *New Statistical Account* state that the old church of Kilmory stood on the farm of Bennicarigan. The foundation stone showed a building of nineteen feet by ten feet, and around it were some ancient gravestones. The graveyard is still in use.

The church was granted to the monks of Kilwinning in 1357, at which time Sir Bean not "Saint Bean," as has been stated ("Sir" was the ordinary title of a priest), was Rector. Kilmory is supposed to have passed to the Hamiltons in 1503.

The present church was built in 1785. Kilmory Well was at one time famous on account of its supposed miraculous healing properties.

SHISKEN CHAPEL

The old chapel or cell of St. Molios stood in the centre of the present graveyard, on the spot now railed in as a grave by the Thomson family. The famous sculptured figure, always supposed to represent St. Molios, stood upon this spot. Mr. Charles Mac Bride of Shedag, who tested the place with a spade some time ago, "came upon stone and lime," as he cautiously puts it. This was probably part of the foundation of the old chapel of the saint.

LOCHRANZA AND CASTLE
From a painting by
J. LAWTON WINGATE, R.S.A.

The sculptured stone has lately been built into the wall of the neighbouring modern church of St. Molios. It represents an abbot with his pastoral staff, holding a chalice in his hands.

The hamlet or clachan of St. Molios, which grew up round his cell, stood on the site of the now dismantled chapel of Kilmichael close by. The position of the old graveyard and ruined church at the entrance to the glen, with the burn in the foreground, is one of the most picturesque and truly old-world sights in Arran.

SANNOX CHAPEL

Of Sannox Chapel there is no vestige left. At the entrance of the beautifully situated graveyard the figure of an ecclesiastic has been built for safety into the stone dike. It is supposed to represent the saint to whom the chapel was dedicated. Even his name is not quite certain, but the place is supposed to have been dedicated to St. Michael, like so many churches in the West Highlands. In the graveyard were buried the remains of

Edwin R. Rose, the young English tourist who was so cruelly murdered by a stranger named Laurie, on Goatfell, in July 1889. A rough boulder-stone covers his grave.

GLEN ASHDALE CHAPEL

There was once a chapel in Glen Ashdale, in size about ten feet by twelve. Both chapel and burial-ground are now almost indistinguishable, like that in Glen Cloy. There were also chapels, as the names suggest, at Kilbride Bennan, at Kilpatrick, at Balnacula (St. Eoin's), at Auchengallon, at Lochranza (St. Bride's), and at Kildonan.

CHAPTER V

ARRAN'S CASTLES

OF old Brodick Castle only one end, and the stones used by the old builders and part of the plan and outline, now remain. It has been practically rebuilt many times, and was completely modernised in the middle of the nineteenth century. None the less, there are few castles can compare with it in associations, and fewer still have been taken and re-taken as often as Brodick. In the re-building of 1844, referred to, a heavy tower was built up on the remains of the old walls, and one winter's night the tower fell with a tremendous crash. Brodick's chief interest lies now in its splendid position and its associations with a hundred wild forays, with fire and with sword. Among the keepers of Arran Castle have been—

A.D.

1296 (about)	Sir John Stewart of Menteith.
1305 (about)	Thomas Bisset of the Glens, in Ireland, and of Rathlin.
1306	Sir John Hastings.
1313	Sir John Stewart of Menteith.
1445	William Stewart (nephew of Robert II.).
1488	Hugh, Lord Montgomery.
1526	George Tait.
1579	Ninian Stewart.
1586	Patrick Hamilton.
1588	Paul Hamilton.

LOCHRANZA CASTLE

One of the finest sights in the West Highlands is the old royal castle of Lochranza, standing, superbly set, on its narrow peninsula of sand, with the water at its feet and the crags above, and all the wealth of reds and browns of the sea margin giving the place its wonderful colouring. The cottages and hills and distant view down Glen Chamadale add another interest to a picture already wild and lovely.

The castle, once a royal residence or hunting lodge, is now in ruins, though only one hundred and forty years ago it was seemingly quite habitable. Its plan is that of a typical Scottish castle, rather better than the mere peel tower. On the first floor the hall measured some 74 ft. by 23 ft., and was lit by three windows. The floor was boarded, at any rate in later times. The castle possessed the luxury of a kitchen, and on the first floor was also another room. The place is mentioned by Fordun in 1400. It was given by John of Menteith to Duncan Campbell of Lochawe in 1433, and in 1445 was occupied by Ronald MacAllister as Captain, at which time he was also tenant of certain crown lands in the island, for which he paid a rent of £16, 6s. 8d., and twelve bolls of bear. As Donal Balloch had about this time laid his lands waste, MacAllister refused to pay his rent. The castle and lands of Lochranza, Cattadell, the two Tonregeys (now barbarously called Thundergay), and other lands were given by James II. to Alexander, Lord Montgomery. His grandson was created Earl of Eglinton, and in 1488 was keeper of Brodick Castle. In 1661 it was still in the possession of the same family. In 1685 it passed to the Montgomeries of Skelmorlie, and early in the next century passed to the Hamiltons.

The chapel of St. Bride, mentioned by Scott as possessing a convent, where dwelt Isabel and the Maid of Lorne, stood on the beach, but not a trace now remains to show the spot.

THE GEOLOGY OF ARRAN

Arran has been said to be in itself an epitome of geology, and in that respect it is unique. Briefly, the Devonian sandstone extends from the east to some five miles inland, and from Brodick takes a turn to the southwest. Trap-rock and carboniferous strata occur in the west and centre of the island. The central granite portion includes the great hills of Goatfell, Cir Mhor and Casteal Abhail. On the north-east and south the granite is joined by mica slate; on the south-east and north by lower Silurian rocks, which are met on the east and south by Devonian sandstone, while lias and oolite lie above the mica slate.

CHAPTER VI

THE CAVES OF ARRAN

FINGAL'S CAVE

CLOSE to the great fort at Drumadoon is the famous cave at the base of the hill known as Tor an Righ, or King's Hill, which the sea has worn out of the sandstone. The roof is arched, and the place lofty and spacious, and on the walls are primitive drawings of dogs and horses engaged in the chase, probably dating from prehistoric times, and, according to tradition, intended to represent Fion. In this cave also Bruce and his followers found shelter during their wanderings in the island, and there are the "King's kitchen," stable, and larder.

THE PREACHING CAVE AT KILPATRICK

Enough of fame attaches to the great cave at Drumadoon, for has it not sheltered both the gods in the person of Fion and his friends, and kings in the person of Bruce? Has it not also been of service to common humanity in sheltering many a keg of good spirits, many a bale of good silk, many a pound of fragrant tobacco? Has it not seen more than one tussle between the men of the Revenue cutters which sailed up and down watching the audacious smugglers of Arran and Kintyre? Was not a daring member of the Clan Innain shot somewhere in these parts in an encounter of the kind? So Drumadoon, having served all classes, gods, kings, lords, and commons, need not usurp the glory of the cave in which another member of the Clan MacKinnon made his mark as one of the many noted preachers of Arran. In this cave Mr. Peter Craig, a man greatly liked for his ability and his geniality, held a school for many years which rivalled that of the village schoolmaster, and turned out many good scholars, who afterwards filled important positions in Glasgow and other towns.

The Preaching Cave was also sometimes used for the ordinary Sunday services.

Largest of all the Arran caves is that known as the Monster Cave at Bennan Head, which has also been used for religious services at different times. Many ancient stone implements and other remains of primitive life have been found amongst the rubbish on the floor of this place.

The early Scottish missionaries made use of many of the caves of the West Highlands as dwelling-places, and it has been suggested by Mr. Lyteill that the word "Piper's" cave so often applied to them is really the word Pypar, a priest. The dog and piper story which we have all heard would thus probably have arisen from the supposition that the word referred to the ordinary profane piper.

THE WONDROUS BAUL OF SAINT MULUY

Martin, in his *Western Islands*, published in 1703, gives a description of the famous healing-stone which is still preserved by the Crawford family. Martin says: "I had like to have forgot a valuable curiosity in this isle, which they call 'Baul muluy,' *i.e.* Molingus, his

Stone Globe. This saint was Chaplain to MackDonald of the Isles; his name is celebrated here on account of this Globe, so much esteemed by the inhabitants. This stone, for its intrinsic value, has been carefully transmitted to posterity for several ages. It is a green stone, much like a globe in figure, about the bigness of a goose egg. The virtues of it is to remove stitches from the sides of sick persons, by laying it close to the place affected, and if the patient does not outlive the distemper they say the stone moves out of the bed of its own accord, and *e contra*. The natives use this stone for swearing decisive oaths upon it. They ascribe another extraordinary virtue to it, and 'tis this—the credulous vulgar firmly believe that if this stone is cast among the front of an enemy they will all run away, and that as often as the enemy rallies, if this stone is cast among them, they will lose courage and retire.

"They say that MackDonald of the Isles carried this stone about him, and that victory was always on his side when he threw it among the enemy. The custody of this globe is the peculiar privilege of a little family called Clan Chattons, *alias* MackIntosh. They were ancient followers of MackDonald of the Isles. This stone is now in the custody of Margaret Miller, *alias* MackIntosh. She lives at Bellmianich, and preserves the globe with abundance of care. It is wrapped in a fair linen cloath, and about that there is a piece of woollen cloath, and she keeps it still locked up in her chest, when it is not given out to exert its qualities."

One has to be careful of these things, and it is well to note that the ball has one serious disadvantage, which those who may wish to avail themselves of its healing qualities should keep in remembrance, else they might be regarded as guilty of manslaughter or worse. It is that, when the person who carries the globe enters the house of the sick person, the first living thing that crosses the line of his path must die, whether it be as small as a butterfly or as large as the ploughman and four horses who, happening to get into the same latitude, fell down dead in Glen Scorra some time since.

It is a little discouraging to know that the globe is somewhat damaged through misadventure, showing clearly that the physician had not power to heal itself.

As to its quality in aiding swearing it is also a little out of date, and we doubt a week in Cowcaddens, the Candlerigs, or in Whitechapel would fit one out with a fuller vocabulary than even Baul Muluy.

PART III
ARRAN IN THE EIGHTEENTH CENTURY

CHAPTER VII

THAT I WERE THERE! *

ROOFLESS the walls and all around is dreary,
    Cold the ingle-side and bare,
Men called it home, 'tis now the wild bird's eyrie,
    Yet I would that I were there!

Just to feel the wild wet breezes swirling
    O'er the water and the whin,
To see the peat-reek o'er the cottage curling
    And the hairst folk winning in.

To see the glens in Autumn's colours tender,
    And the black Ben's misty wreath,
The birk and the breckan's dying splendour,
    And the roaring linn beneath.

To see the foam from the white beach flying
    And the boats leap through the waves,
And the ring of golden sea-tang lying
    Strayed from Atlantic's caves.

To hear again the beach-nuts falling, falling,
    When the plantin's winning bare,
To hear again the paitricks calling, calling,
    Oh, would that I were there!

M'K. M'B.

* *With acknowledgments to " The Spectator."*

ARRAN IN THE EIGHTEENTH CENTURY

THE OLD RUNRIG SYSTEM

AT the beginning of the eighteenth century Arran was in much the same condition as the rest of the Highlands: the men tilled the lands of their forefathers and ate the crops they grew. They fished and shot game without hindrance,* and the chiefs were more anxious that there should exist on the land a hardy race of strong men who could wield a claymore than to know what he received in bolls of meal from the "kindly tenants" of the lordship. The whole idea of Highland life was in most districts still patriarchal: the Highland chief had not developed into the modern landlord.

In places like Arran, Bute, and Kintyre, there was seldom a scarcity of food, and the men of these parts possessed exceptional hardihood. In Arran and Kintyre especially, the old stories of feats of strength were plentiful twenty years ago. Mr. Neil Munro has

---

*See the present writer's paper on *The Rights of the Individual under the Clan System.*

OLD BRIDGE: NORTH GLEN SENNOX
From a painting by
J. LAWTON WINGATE, R.S.A.

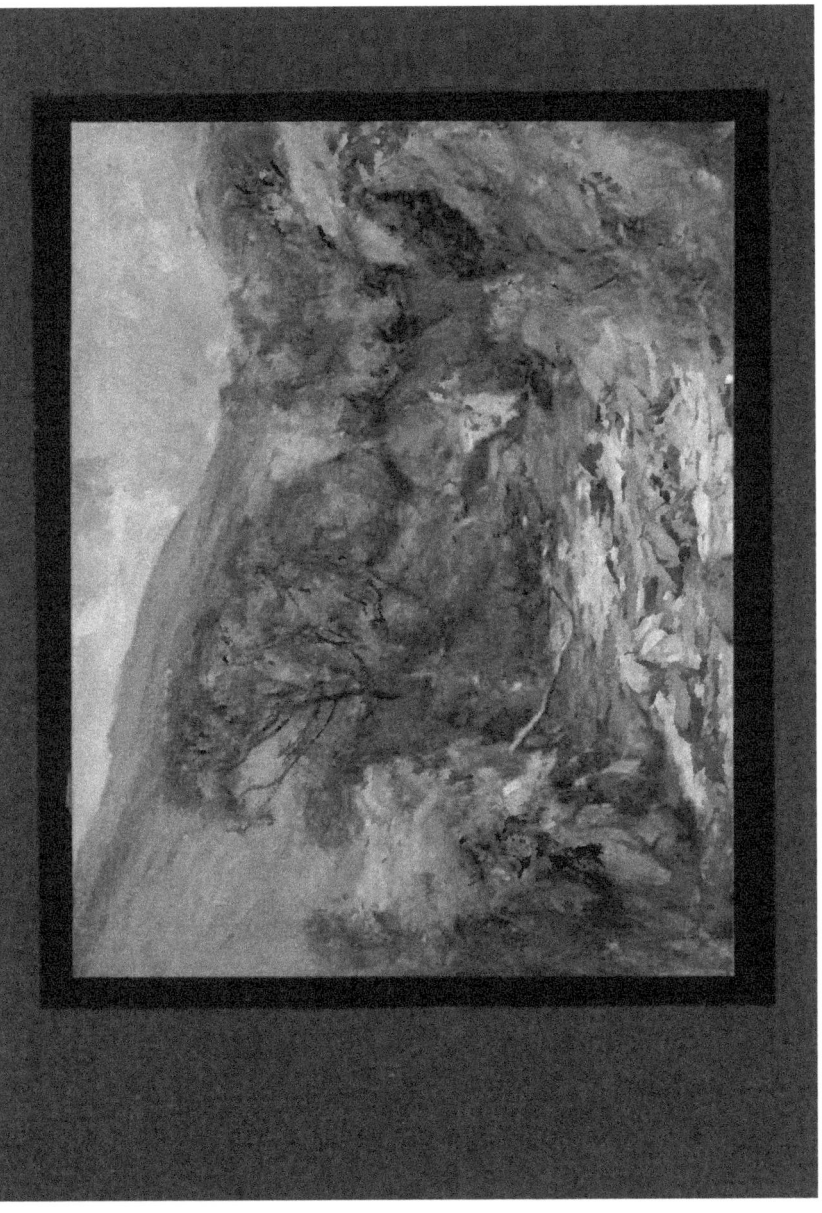

given us an interesting, and I think well-considered, picture of the mainland of Argyll fifty to seventy years earlier in his *John Splendid*, showing that the conditions of life as regards food were eminently suitable for the rearing of strong men and women. It is true that some of the Highland lairds, who held by the charter rather than by the sword, attempted to maintain a semi-feudal state of things, and had become aggressive, but they were the exception, and it seems to me that even the occasional tyranny of these men was better than the purely commercial relations between rich and poor, chief and clansman, which came into existence after the long absence of the attainted chiefs who took part in the Rising of 1745. Recently published letters show the intimate relations which existed in old times between the rich and poor, the chief and his clansmen, and the great difference that followed upon the return of the chiefs.

The late Mr. Patrick Murray thus describes the rise in the value of land which was then taking place in Scotland and

England, due to the growth of industry and other causes :—

"The country assumed a settled condition to which it had long been strange. The first of our countrymen began to return from the Indies with fortunes acquired in our possessions there—new life was given to industry and enterprise of every kind, and the trade of Glasgow and the country generally made a fresh and vigorous start. As a consequence of all this the price of land rose considerably from the low level at which it had long stood, and landlords in different parts of Scotland took to farming on new and improved methods. Although it may seem strange now, these were introduced from England, and English servants and implements of husbandry were brought to Scotland for this purpose. Lord Eglinton was one of the first in this part of the country to set the example on a large scale, and his English servants introduced drill husbandry and the culture of turnips into Ayrshire. At the peace of 1763 large fortunes made during the war with great rapidity were brought home and invested in land, and money diffused itself amongst all classes. The price of corn rose at least one-third. The price of cattle, which had almost doubled in the previous thirty years, rose in 1766 still higher. Farming and improvements became the fashion, and every country gentleman took to them on a greater or less scale.

"The farms were let on leases of nineteen years' duration, and at their entry to them the tenants had paid a grassum, which was the last of this custom in Arran. These leases began to expire in 1766, the greater part of them falling out in 1772. In view of this, the tutors of the Duke of Hamilton, who was then a minor, determined to set about the improvement of the island, and appointed Mr. John Burrell, their factor at Kinneil, to reset the tacks and to advise the measures to be adopted for improvement, and to direct the operations resolved on."

JOHN BURRELL

This man played an important part in the later history of Arran. He was, judging by name, probably English or of English origin. He was a perfect stranger, at any rate, and there is no one like a stranger for the work if you want the old landmarks removed, for a stranger knows no traditions, feels no sentimental scruples. This the Highland landlords realised perfectly a little later when they wished to evict the old tillers of the soil to make room for sheep or deer.

Mr. Murray says: "In carrying out his commission Mr. Burrell visited Arran from 1766 to 1782, at least nine times, for periods ranging from one to four months. He made what he calls a 'strict survey' of every farm, and reported fully his whole doings in the island.

HIS SCHEME OF IMPROVEMENT

"Of all his schemes, the most important was the making of enclosures, on which work large sums were spent by the proprietor on his recommendation. An overseer and workmen were brought from the mainland to make the dikes on several farms as a sample of what was wanted, and afterwards the tenants them-

selves were encouraged to do the work.
Forty spades were ordered from Ayrshire to
begin with, but Arran smiths were allowed
to try their hands on more. The old turf
dykes which are still to be seen in the island,
some of them outside the limits of the arable
land, are part of those laid out by Mr. Burrell
at this time. Those at Drumadoon and at
Torbeg and Tormore were some of the first
made, and also those at Blairbeg, but in re-
setting the tacks a certain amount was stipulated to be done on every farm at the
proprietor's expense. He opened the lime
quarry in the Clachan Glen, and also the
slate quarry at Lochranza. He made a
trial for coal at the Cock Farm, and put down
a bore at Clauchlands. He inveighed against
the barbarous system of runrig and rundale
which the tenantry of the Island of Arran
were so fond of. He lamented the extrava-
gant number of horses kept by the tenants,
and ordered that a plough and oxen should
be sent to the island, and a premium given to
the tenant who first ploughed his land with
oxen. In short, to quote his own words—

'Many a serious thought and contemplation the memorialist has bestowed upon the cultivation and improvement of this island which had the effect to produce many a different idea.'"

The older families had exceptional rights, many of them the remains of their original proprietorship or of privileges granted long ago to their ancestors. Mr. Burrell introduced new men from Argyll and the low country, and gave them the same rights and privileges, or rather restricted the old rights to the same level as those granted to the new-comers, naturally causing much heartburning and discontent amongst the old clans of the island.

THE GREAT REVOLUTION

"At that time," Mr. Murray says, "farms in the island were arranged so that the whole were out of lease at one time in the year 1776. This was done to admit of rectification of marches and a better division of the farms and of the interior or hill grazings. . . . This, we may be sure, was a serious enough business for both parties, but it did not altogether take the heart out of the tenants."

Of course the greatest revolution Mr. Burrell effected was in the conversion of the old runrig farms into lots or separate holdings. By the runrig system the farm was cultivated in strips by four to ten or more tenants, generally of the same family. The strips changed hands every two years. The plan was interesting, and essentially communistic in character. Mr. Burrell viewed it with horror, though it really stood upon a higher moral basis than the competitive method which followed. Nor was there anything inherently bad in it commercially, or need why it should fail, *provided the farm and the individual strips were large enough to support the men who tilled them.*

So far from reflecting upon the intelligence of the men who adopted it, as Mr. Burrell and Mr. Murray thought it did, the runrig system was based on a principle on which we are acting little by little to-day— the principle of real co-operation. Loudon says of it: "Absurd as the common field system is at this day, it was admirably suited to the circumstances in which it originated, the plan having been conceived in wisdom, and executed with extraordinary accuracy."

A kind of administrative committee, which was formed apparently by Mr. Burrell himself in 1770, included the following members: John Burrell, George Couper, William MacGregor, Patrick Hamilton, John Hamilton, Gershom Stewart (minister of Kilbride), Duncan MacBride, John Pette, John Fullarton, Gavin Fullarton, John Hamilton, Thomas Brown, William Ogg, Hector MacAllister, Alexander MacGregor, John MacCook, and Adam Fullarton. Of these at least four were directly or indirectly employed by the Arran estate manager, while ten of the whole number were dependent on the Hamilton interest, and bound to support Mr. Burrell's measures; so that this committee cannot be taken as a popularly representative one for the whole island, anything of the nature of popular government being as yet unknown.

The chief matter discussed was the question of a scheme for a service of packet boats run-

IN THE EIGHTEENTH CENTURY

ning between the island and Saltcoats. Other matters decided by the committee were—

Rogue and road money, and statute labour on the roads.

The suming and rouming of the island, which was immediately carried into execution.

Tenants to keep herds and to fold their cattle every night, according to Act of Parliament.

Multures to be commuted for a fixed payment per boll meal for grinding.

Sheep to be marked, and no cattle or sheep to be killed without calling together a jury of the three nearest neighbours.

All weights and measures to be taken to the castle, and compared with Ayr weights and measures.

With a view to encouraging improvements in husbandry in 1776, premiums were offered to the tenants as follows :—

To the tenant who shall produce the best three-year-old humbled bull of his own property, not under the value of £10 stg.—5 guineas.

To the tenant who shall produce the best two-year-old tup of Bakewell and Chaplin kind—full blood—not under the value of £5 stg.—2½ guineas.

To the tenant who shall produce the best three-year-old entire horse, not under the value of £15 stg., and not above 15 hands high—7½ guineas.

To the tenant who shall have the best field of turnips, not under 3 acres, sown broad-cast after a summer fallow by 3 ploughings, and manured—6 guineas. And to him who shall have the best field not under 3 acres, in drills 2½ feet distance, horsehoed no less than 3 times, and the ground well manured—5 guineas.

To the tenant who shall have the best field of cabbages, not less than 2 acres, well prepared, planted at 4 feet distance 'twixt rows, and 1½ feet distance in the rows, which will take about 20,000 plants—to be three times horsehoed (which, at 4 lbs. a plant, will fatten in 9 weeks 16 head of cattle, which should sell at £3 advance, or £24 an acre)—shall have 6 guineas.

To the tenant who shall have the first 10 acres enclosure finished in terms of the articles—5 guineas.

To the tenant who shall have the greatest quantity and best quality of wheat upon enclosed ground, and after a thorough summer fallow of 5 furrows, sufficiently manured, and no less than 2 acres—2 guineas.

To the tenant who shall have the greatest quantity of clover and rye-grass hay from at least 2 acres, sown with barley or wheat, after summer fallow, of 5 furrows, and properly manured, and not less than 100 stones an acre, and upon enclosed ground—2 guineas.

Amongst the prize-winners in the two years following were Angus MacKillop, Alexander Thomson, Patrick Crawford, Robert Shaw, John Currie, and Alexander MacKinnon.

The Duke also obtained the services of an experienced fisherman, one Andrew Wilson, to teach the art of line fishing to any of the islanders who applied to him.

SMUGGLING IN ARRAN

As on other parts of the coast, at this time a good deal of money was made by the natives

IN THE EIGHTEENTH CENTURY 51

out of smuggling—possibly more than was in many cases made out of their crofts. Mr. Murray says: " No notice of Arran at this time is possible without a reference to the making and smuggling of the famous 'Arran water.' In spite of gaugers, excise officers, and frequent seizures of malt and whisky, it was persevered in. As the Arran people are pre-eminently law-abiding, I can only account for this peculiarity on the supposition that the product of their stills was so very good that they could not find it in their hearts to believe that any law could make the making of it bad. I find a list of 32 stills in Arran in 1784, of which 23 were in the south end. In that year an Act of Parliament was passed for the licensing of small stills in the Highlands of Scotland, by which proprietors were made liable, along with their tenants, for the heavy fines imposed in case of the latter being convicted of illicit distillation. After the passing of the Act 26 stills were collected and carried to the Castle. In 1797, when illicit distillation would appear to have been at its height, a letter from Arran describes whisky as a perfect drug in the market—it being supposed there were no less than 50 stills at the south end of the island. At that time the whole annual produce of bere (from 500 to 2000 quarters), would appear to have been used in the Island for distilling. It suffered no decrease until, in the early years of the nineteenth century, the Duke of Hamilton threatened to dispossess any tenant convicted of illicit distillation, and from that time it appears to have decreased, and then disappeared entirely. In the malt kiln, the ruins of which are still standing in the grounds of the Whitehouse, there was a licensed still of the capacity of forty gallons, from which, from December 1793 to November 1794, whisky was sold to the amount of £500 at 2s. per Scotch pint, or 4s. per gallon."

Every one, including the Duke and Mr. Burrell, was shocked at the smuggling, and for it the islanders were roundly abused by the ministers.

FAMOUS ARRAN PREACHERS

It must not be supposed from this, however, that Arran was a drunken island. Mr. Paterson, writing in 1830, says emphatically that it was not so, and Arran was prolific in preachers. The Rev. J. Kennedy Cameron says in his *Memoir of the Rev. John MacAllister*: "Smuggling was common in Arran at that time, and John MacAlister took his share in smuggling adventures like the rest. But a religious revival arose in Kilmorie, under the preaching of the parish minister, the Rev. Neil MacBride, and among the awakened people were Angus MacMillan, Finlay and Archibald Cook, Peter Davidson, Archibald Nicol, and John MacAlister—men who afterwards attained a great deal of religious influence throughout the Highlands."

And of course Arran was not the only place in which there was smuggling. It was carried on also in Kintyre and Galloway, and on every other coast of Scotland, including Mr. Burrell's own neighbourhood of the Forth! In the Essex district, to which reference has been made, it went on to an enormous extent, the houses of the wealthy, and even the very churches, being used as storehouses in which to hide spirits and other smuggled articles.

So that, though we can appreciate the valuable picture Mr. Burrell's diary gives us of the Arran of his day, we must remember that it was impossible for him to view things from the native's point of view. He supplies us with the facts, but we must ourselves put in the pinches of salt if we would get at the truth, without doing injustice to the men of our own hearths who lived through that time of revolution and bitter disillusionment in Arran and the Highlands generally.

For example, Mr. Burrell shows that husbandry was old-fashioned and poor, that there were no proper roads in the modern sense, that the bridges were of wood, the connection with the mainland irregular, letters being delivered haphazard as opportunity offered. That the boat fare to Ayr was 15s., that the boats were badly constructed and deficient in the matter of tackle, and that the whole of the island, save the park of Brodick Castle, was unenclosed.

But of course we must not assume that

Arran was the only place without roads, or was necessarily behind very many, if not most, other districts of England and Scotland.

We are told that the first manure ever applied to land in Ayrshire was in 1758 and 1760. In Essex we read of a road having been ploughed with the object of levelling the ruts; and that in 1768 "no road ever equalled that from Billericay to the King's Head at Tilbury. It is for nearly twelve miles so narrow that a mouse cannot pass by any carriage. . . . The ruts are of an incredible depth . . . and I must not forget the eternally meeting with chalk-waggons, themselves frequently stuck fast, till a collection of them are in the same situation, and twenty or thirty horses may be tacked to each to draw them out one by one."

Nor were the manners of the people all that could be desired, even in this enlightened county so near London. "The men were notoriously drunken, and the clergy ignorant, intemperate, and neglectful. It is said that the farmers who met at a certain Rochford hostelry used to set a hen on their arrival, and would continue their drinking bout until the chickens were hatched."*

Very different is the description of the Arran people given by Pennant and by Paterson, a later factor of the island, who says: "In moral character the people of Arran . . . are hospitable amongst themselves and to strangers. They are more confiding in each other than is altogether prudent. The money and other property of the more fortunate among them are freely lent to those in need, often when there is but a slight prospect of repayment. To their aged and infirm relations they are generally kind and dutiful, and scarcely any are ever allowed to beg their bread. . . . The people of Arran may justly be described as a religious community . . . so far as recollected, there is not a single native who can with justice be called a drunkard."

It would have been well if those later writers upon Arran, like the Rev. Mr. MacArthur, who talk of the introduction amongst its people of "the more practical and enlight-

* *Rambles round Southend*, by the present writer.

CORN CUTTING
From a painting by
J. LAWTON WINGATE, R.S.A.

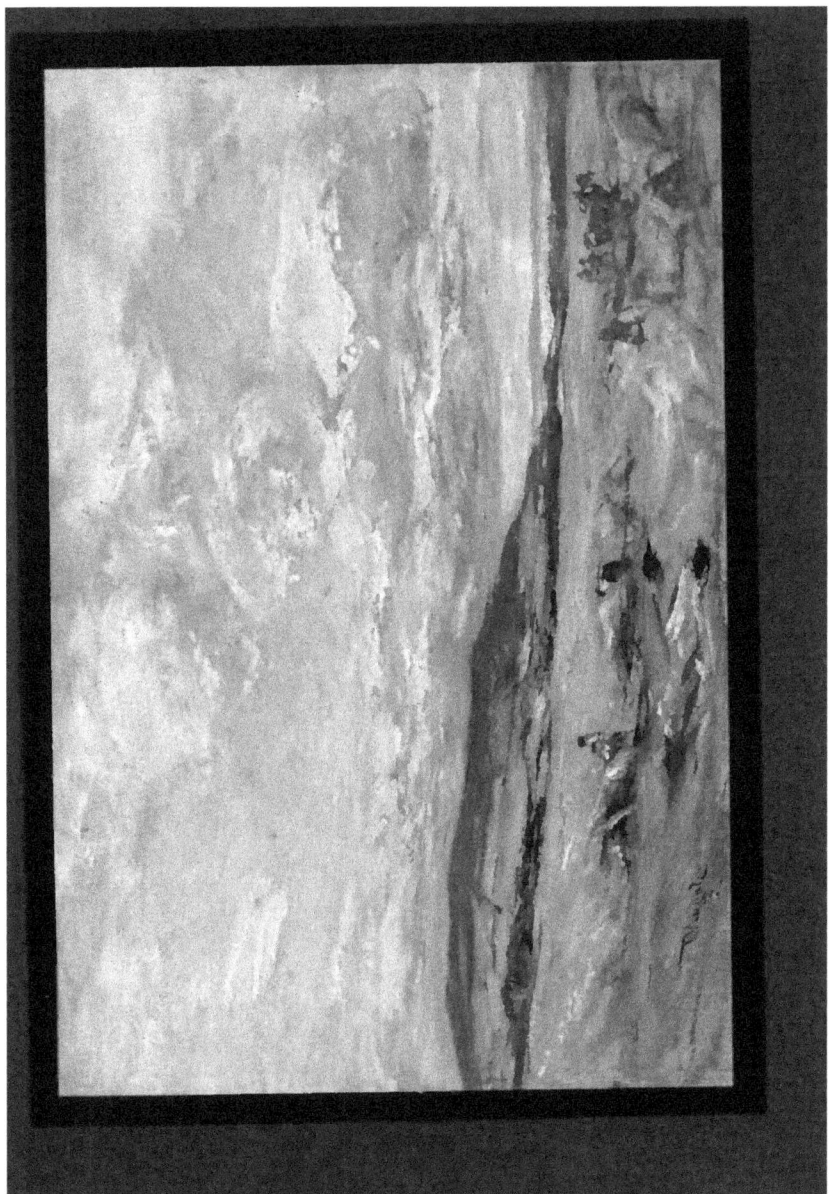

ened views of their lowland neighbours," had looked round to see what their lowland and English neighbours actually did before making their unkind reflections.

THE ARRAN EVICTIONS

Mr. Burrell was a man of exceptional ability, and introduced many valuable agricultural reforms, but his hand was undoubtedly against the natives, and the inevitable result of the "lotting" of the island into large farms and the restriction of the hill grazings, was that wholesale evictions followed about the year 1812 to 1815. Again, about the year 1821, it is stated that 500 persons were sent away chiefly from the Sannox district. About half the passage money was paid by the Duke, who also obtained for them grants of land from Government amounting to 100 acres per family. Many of the people settled in lower Canada and Chaleur Bay. The Rev. Alexander MacBride states in his *New Statistical Account of Kilmory*, that many of the ejected families emigrated to North

America but by far the greater number removed to Ayrshire towns.

But long prior to this, in 1770, five years after Mr. Burrell's advent, the people were leaving the old home which was undergoing so radical an alteration. In that year Burrell considers that it was dangerous to suspend the "Baron" Court for six months, "finding that so many people intending for America, to leave the place at the time without a judge would be leaving it in the power of these emigrants to rob both his grace and their neighbours."

The suggestion that Highlanders would at that time rob their own unfortunate kinsfolk, when themselves broken-hearted at the prospect of leaving all they knew and loved, seems wanton and without justification in fact or precedent. It is fortunately clear from his own arrangement made previously, to defer the sitting of the Baron Court for six months (which he thus wished to alter), that the men of Arran could not have been other than the quiet, law-abiding folk visitors find them to-day. Imagine us in 1910 deferring the sittings of a court for six months in a community of six thousand persons!

Of course bitter feelings and keen opposition were aroused by the revolutionary changes, just as in the years following the introduction of the black-faced sheep (from about 1790) and the consequent clearing of the Sannox district, we are told by another able and not unkindly factor of the estate, John Paterson, that the people "opposed the changes in every way short of physical resistance." It is made clear in the "Diary" that Burrell's stern and iconoclastic measures had roused the people to hatred and despair, and he complains of them plotting against the Duke.

Whatever else they accomplished, Mr. Burrell's efforts do not seem to have improved the comfort of the people, for we are told that about 1810 the condition of all save the few big tacksmen was miserable, that their houses were the meanest hovels, while they were clad in the coarsest garments of home manufacture.

It seems that, as happened with the introduction of purely commercial methods into England, the people were robbed of many privileges and perquisites which they had long regarded as their own. Their condition thus became worse than it was in 1766, when the changes commenced, though it is pretended by Mr. MacArthur and others that in the Highlands all good things followed the introduction of modern methods after the Forty-five, when strangers of Mr. Burrell's type were set to work to "reform" the Highlands by reducing men and things therein to what Mr. Cunningham Graham would call their "lowest common multiple"—the principle of commercialism. In this work it is to be feared that many of the old ministers unconsciously lent a hand, by their efforts to beat the harmless and already well-cudgelled natives into "reform." For in their ardour they were unable to discriminate between those customs that lent gaiety and brightness to Highland life, and were in themselves a valuable possession which made for refinement, and those which were really harmful.

WHAT PENNANT SAW

Pennant, an Englishman, writing in 1776, or just ten years after Mr. Burrell was sent to modernise Arran, says: "The men (of Arran) are strong, tall, and well made . . . all speak the Erse language. Their diet is chiefly potatoes and meal, and during winter some dried mutton or goat is added to their hard fare. A deep dejection appears in general through the countenances of all: no time can be spared for amusement of any kind, the whole being given for procuring the means of paying their rent, of laying in their fuel, or getting in a scanty pittance of meat and clothing." Pennant, in 1771, again points out that the farms were "set by roup or auction, and advanced by unnatural force to above double the old rent." He says further that "the late rents were scarce £1200 a year; the expected rents £3000."

The actual rent-roll of the island in the year 1778 was roundly, according to Mr. Burrell's own figures, £5550, or with some additions £5880.

From this it will be seen how greatly his

efforts had improved his employer's property, and had stimulated the rent-roll, while they had ruined and impoverished the lives of the people.

As a contrast to the description of the Arran islanders by Pennant above quoted, may be taken his description of the songs, the gaiety, the pleasant lore, and the colour generally by which life in the Highlands had been everywhere characterised. Describing the Island of Skye in the same year he says : " They sing in the same manner when they are cutting down the corn, when thirty or forty join in chorus, keeping time to the sound of a bagpipe, as the Grecian lasses were wont to do to that of a lyre during the vintage in the days of Homer. The subject of the songs at the Luaghadh, the Quern, and on this occasion, are sometimes love, sometimes panegyric, and often a rehearsal of the deeds of the ancient heroes." All these things, surely a splendid inheritance and worth preserving, surely a fine contrast to the silly songs of the music-halls of Glasgow and London, have gone, swept away in the desire to modernise and get more money out of life instead of gaiety, refinement, good feeling, character.

I have heard it stated that in Sannox the people were evicted because there had been so much intermarrying that there were great numbers of deaf and dumb persons in the villages! I have not, however, found any justification for this statement. There was in Arran generally, as there is in all country districts, a certain amount of intermarrying, but it does not appear to have been commoner than in any other part of Scotland, nor than in English rural districts, and it was certainly less common than in Norway and many other parts of the Continent. My judgment is based upon a list of the surnames then in Sannox, many of which were those of comparatively new-comers, and not of Arran origin. In view of the nearness of the island to Kintyre, Bute, the mainland of Argyll, and to Renfrewshire and Ayrshire, I doubt much whether the intermarrying has at any time been great enough to affect the health and physique of the people in the slightest degree.

The fact is, that the people stood in the

way of huge farms, of the deer, the sheep, and of absolute ownership; as Mr. Somerville of Lochgilphead, quoted by MacKenzie,* said of that time: "The watchword of all is exterminate, exterminate the native race. Through this monomania of landlords the cottar population is all but extinct, and the substantial yeomen is undergoing the same process of dissolution." To give an example, "On the west side of Loch Awe," MacKenzie says, "once forty-five families were maintained; the place is now rented by a single sheep farmer."

Dr. Donald MacLeod, writing in 1863, said, "Is not a man better than sheep? They who would have shed their blood like water for Queen and country are in other lands, Highland still, but expatriated for ever."

> If you want men to-day,
>   Pipe you never so loudly,
> No lads come away
>   With their cheeks glowing proudly;
> You may call on the deer,
>   On the grouse and grey wether,
> But *not* on the lads
>   With the bonnet and feather:

* *History of the Highland Clearances.*

> When you called to the fight
> Then they ever were ready,
> They, light-hearted and gay,
> They, the strong and the steady!

ARRAN AND THE FORTY-FIVE

The Hamiltons are said by Mr. Andrew Lang not to have been on the side of the Stuarts at the time of the famous rising, but Mr. James MacBride, writer (of Glasgow), states that his great-grandfather, James MacGregor, was sent by the duke with a letter to Prince Charles. When MacGregor, whose papers seem to confirm this story, reached the prince, he was at Culloden, and seeing that the letter could now only bring certain trouble to his chief, he took it back to the duke, who was pleased with his shrewdness. Years after, when MacGregor was about to be ejected from his farm at Clachan, by the side of the old graveyard of Shisken, he wrote a letter to the duke, which is still, I understand, preserved, in which he appealed against the factor's action in ejecting him, and reminded him in guarded language of the service he had rendered years before. MacGregor, a fiery and outspoken old Highlander, and his brother, came from Bracklin, and were at one time high in the duke's favour.

Mr. MacBride, who tells the story, is the grand old man of Arran, being over ninety years of age. He is as handsome, as rosy cheeked, and as alert as a man of sixty, and still goes down to his business every morning at nine o'clock and discusses his clients' causes, or, in unoccupied moments, will crack over old Arran memories with much enthusiasm.

The writer of the *New Statistical Account of Kilmory* states that the Hon. Charles Boyle, son of Lord Kilmarnock, fled, like his ancestors had done in Bruce's time, to Arran, and lay concealed in the farm of Auchaleffan till he found a chance of getting across to France. This, says the writer, was the Mr. Boyle who received Dr. Johnson at Slanes Castle many years later.

PART IV
THE BRANDANI

CHAPTER VIII

OLD FAMILIES IN ARRAN

THE ARRAN AND BUTE BARONS

ON the mainland of Scotland, highland and lowland, the old historic names have gradually been rooted out, just as in England the old " Statesmen " of Westmorland and Cumberland have been bought or sold out by the few great landholders. The whole tendency has been for the possession of the land to become concentrated in the hands of a very few. The Johnstones no longer hold Annandale as "kindly tenants" or small lairds ; the Galloway clans are mixed up with the rest of the community ; the lairds of Kintyre might be numbered on your fingers; and the MacVicars, Munros, MacNicols, MacKellars, MacInturners, and others have long disappeared from Loch Fyne. The very names have in many cases vanished, and all the old traditions of the countryside which they inherited from their fathers have gone with them.

In Arran and in Bute things were somewhat different, and as reward for service rendered to the Bruces and the Stewarts the old Brandani were supported in their possessions by the kings to which the two islands belonged from time to time. At the date of the Bute charter of 1506 the Butemen are shown to have been possessed of lands, and there is every reason to believe that the people of Arran, with whom they had been closely associated in all their exploits, held, in an identical manner, the lands which they had probably first received from the Somerledian chiefs, the design of Robert Bruce to keep the islands as a recruiting ground for the Scottish army being clearly shown in his will.

So it has happened that amongst the people of Arran and Bute are still represented the old Barons, who date from the days of Bruce and Robert II., and in many cases from the time of Somerled. The old Gaelic proverb says: "Clann Bhridean agus clann Ennain, na cloinne a's sìne ann an Arrinn," and amongst the old names are also MacLouie (MacLoy or Fullarton), MacCook (in Gaelic, MacCug), MacDavid or Davidson, MacGilker, MacAllister, Stewart, Hunter, Kelso, Kerr, Kennedy, MacMhurrich or MacVurich (which has been whittled down to Murchie and Currie), MacMaster, Brown (MacBraon or MacBrayne), MacNicol, Love, Crawford, Hamilton, MacNish, while MacMillan, MacKillop, MacKenzie, Shaw, Thomson, Robertson, Bannatyne, and MacKelvie are later but yet old names in the island. Nearly all these families are still represented in Arran, though their names date back longer than those of half the members of the House of Lords.

Mr. Patrick Murray, late factor of the Arran estates, writing in 1890, says: "One thing I have had brought home to me in looking back over these old records is the frequency with which I recognise names in the rental of to-day in that of one hundred years ago. In some cases the same names—both surname and Christian—appear in the very same farms as they did last century. Any of these Arran tenants I refer to would have no difficulty in compiling their pedigree for the Herald's College whenever that should be wanted."

In Arran and Bute the relations between chief and people had in old times been exceptionally close, as will be seen by the account of the Battle of the Stones in another chapter. There had long been a middle class of gentry in both islands. A visitor to the island in 1628 says: "Neither is there any isle like to it for brave gentry, good archers, and hill-hovering hunters." These were, it seems from the surnames, originally descendants of Somerled, like the MacBrides, MacKirdys, MacAllisters, and Bannatynes, and of officers and others attached to the household of Somerled, like the MacKinnons, MacVurichs, and probably the MacCugs, Hunters, and also the MacGilchattans and MacGildowies, who seem to have originated in Kintyre.

According to the tradition, at the time of Bruce, they were confirmed in their possessions, and got new grants, while later the

OLD ARRAN HOUSES, WHITING BAY
From a painting by
J. LAWTON WINGATE, R.S.A.

Stewarts and others joined their ranks; their duty was to provide a force of twenty-four men to form the king's bodyguard. They certainly were transferred with all their rights on the passing of the island of Arran to the Lord Hamilton, who had married the king's sister, Jane. In the sixteenth century, as is shown by historical documents, they seem to have held by military service of the Hamiltons. The old tradition is that the holders of the charters, which the older generation of Arran men affirm were identical with those granted to MacLouie, got into debt owing to the small annual tribute to the superior not having been claimed for many years, and that the Hamilton family impounded the charters. Be that as it may, it is certain that the descendants of these men were called "Baron" within the recollections of persons now living, and this title was used only by military tenants of the Crown. The Rev. Neil MacBride of Lamlash, a nephew of the Rev. Alexander MacBride, author of the *New Statistical Account of Kilmory Parish*, wrote in 1890: "Bruce's Arran friends who received gifts of land in the island bore the names you have given, as I have often heard, and a descendant of one of them, M'Kinnon, who died at Brodick in my own day, was better known as 'The Baron' than by his own name."

Local tradition is, and has always been, very strong on the point. MacArthur says, writing in 1870: "A few centuries ago the lands of the island were divided amongst several petty chiefs or barons, and standing stones were raised as landmarks to define the boundaries of their possessions, and prevent the encroachment of neighbouring chiefs . . . and among the dells and over the heathery moors these rude monuments of the island chiefs may still be seen, mutely eloquent of the . . . old times. By the roadside between Brodick and Lamlash there stand three massive blocks of red sandstone, which are said to mark the spot where the lands of three of the old proprietors of Arran met." Pennant, who during his stay in the island in 1771 was shown about by the parish minister, Mr. Lindsay, and visited Fullarton of Kilmichael, and no doubt got his information largely

OLD FAMILIES IN ARRAN

from him, says: "Arran was the property of the Crown. Robert Bruce returned thither during his distresses, and met with protection from his faithful vassals. Numbers of them followed his fortunes; and after the battle of Bannockburn he rewarded several, such as the MacCooks, MacKinnons, MacBrides, and MacLouies or Fullartons with different charters of lands in their native country." Other writers add the names of the Stewarts and Hunters to this list.

Pennant goes on to say: "About the year 1334 the island seems to have formed part of the estate of Robert Stewart, Great Steward of Scotland, afterwards Robert II. At that time" (the natives) "took up arms to support the cause of their master, who afterwards, in reward, not only granted at their request an immunity from their annual tribute of corn, but added several new privileges, and a donation to all the inhabitants that were present."

CHAPTER IX

THE BRANDANES
OR, MEN OF ARRAN AND BUTE

I HAVE in the following pages adopted the old name of the islanders, as it is quite impossible in many cases to distinguish between deeds done by the Arran or Butemen singly and those done collectively.

Arnold Blair, chaplain to Wallace, from whose MS. Blind Harry got his material, writing shortly after the death of Wallace, in 1305, says: "In this unfortunate battle (Falkirk) were slain, on the Scottish side, John Stewart of Bute, with his Brandans; for so they name them that are taken up to serve in the wars forth of the Stewart's lands." Both the islands had, it will be remembered, been acquired by the Stewarts a century earlier by the marriage with Jane, granddaughter of Angus MacSomhairle. Hector Boece, writing in 1527, says: "Brandani—ita enim ea ætate incolæ Arain et Boitæ insularum vulgo vocabantur." "The term," says Fullarton, "has been understood as denoting the military tenants holding of the Great Steward"; and this explanation seems to fit in best with all the facts, especially with the evidences of their independent action on many occasions,—an independence worthy of the old Gall Gael of whom they were the descendants. D. Macpherson says: "The people of Bute, and I believe also of Arran, perhaps so called in honour of St. Brendan." St. Brendan, who died in A.D. 577, was a companion of St. Colum or Columba. Camden states that the saint lived and laboured in Bute; but there seems to be no direct evidence of this.

The Rev. Neil MacBride of Lamlash again suggests that the word Brandani means the bold water or spray men; and, of course, it is quite possible that it may mean simply the men of the sea of Brandan. The *Book of Arran* goes, I think, far afield when it follows Captain White, who assumes that the name Kilbrannan refers to a kil or cell of St. Brendan of Clonfert, and tries to find in a small church on the coast of Kintyre the actual cell of this saint. Mr. Balfour, is, I think, equally mistaken in believing that in the site at Kilpatrick they have discovered the real St. Brendan's church. The site, he says, is "on the northern shoulder of Leac Bhreac." The name of the hill that guards it is Torr an Daimh, which he translates "the hill of the church." This is, he says, "the only known memorial save the record furnished by the cashel itself, that this was one of the first outposts of Christianity in Scotland." This site, first discovered by the Arran Society, may, of course, be ecclesiastical, but it does not follow that it was founded by Brendan.

Mr. Balfour asks where, failing this, is the church which gives its name to Kilbrandon Sound?

St. Brendan does not seem to have figured largely in the West Highlands. There is a small parish church in Argyll called Kilbrandon, and my suggestion is that the name of the Sound contains no reference to a church; that the word is not Kil but "Kyle," a narrow sea, passage, or strait of water, which is familiar in the "Kyles" of Bute, the "Kyle" of Lochalsh, "Kulri" in Skye. I suggest that this name was given long before Brendan's time, and is taken from the name Bran or Branan MacLir, a brother of Mannanan, who beyond doubt gave his name to the neighbour isle of Man. They were sons of Ler the sea-god, made famous by Shakespeare, and in the Keltic story, *The Fate of the Children of Lir*. The old name of the islanders, assuming that it contains the same root, the Brandani or Brannani, would be thus the followers of the war-god, a name that would fit their character when history first introduces us to them. By that time Bran had undergone the change which so many of his brother gods underwent when the Christian monks had the shrewdness to appropriate them for their own Church; he was by them credited with having introduced Christianity into Britain, and became Bran the Blessed!

The fact that the name of the saint, though common in Ireland, does not occur amongst the men either of Arran or Kintyre, who are all men of the Sound of Kilbrandon, seems to support my contention, or at any rate to suggest that the saint's and their name have no connection with each other, save that they are probably borrowed from the same source.

It is to be regretted that the Rev. J. K. Hewison in his *Bute in the Olden Time*, unlike any other writer on the subject, has written as though all the deeds of the Brandani had been performed by the Bute men alone, which is as unreasonable as it would be to suppose that Wallace's remark given by Blind Harry—"Good westland men of Arran and Rauchle, if they be warned they will all come to me," did not include in Wallace's mind the men of Bute itself, who with their Arran kinsmen and the men of Fife had fought so splendidly at Falkirk.

CHAPTER X

THE LANGUAGE OF ARRAN

THE original speech of Arran was, of course, Gaelic, which was the common language of conversation amongst the natives till some thirty or forty years ago. That it is now dying out, though still, of course, understood and spoken, is greatly to be regretted, nay, it is sad and shameful. Of course, until the action of the Highland and Scottish Societies of Edinburgh, Glasgow, London, and the Colonies nothing was done for its encouragement, but it has, after a long agitation, now been placed by the Education Department on the same footing as French, or Welsh, or any other language. It remains for the Highland people themselves to insist upon it being properly taught to their children in the elementary schools.

The excuse for neglecting it—the most precious gift the Highlander has received from his cultured ancestors of early Christian times—was that it interfered with the teaching of subjects of commercial value. This supposition has been utterly disproved by many years of actual experience of Welsh teaching, in which it has been shown, as admitted by inspectors, that, so far from the bi-lingual children being behind the others, they are invariably more intelligent, more alert, more advanced generally. And, of course, it is easy to see that it must be so, for the English language is far less opulent, less complex than the Keltic tongues, which are more capable, therefore, of expressing fine shades of thought and meaning.

The vocabulary of the English peasant has been estimated to contain about 400 to 600 words. On the other hand a German philologist, Dr. Finck, some years ago made a study of the language of the Aran islanders on the spot. Dr. Finck took down no less than 4000 words which he found occurring in the daily speech of the inhabitants of that remote Irish island. Dr. Douglas Hyde, commenting on these investigations, wrote at the time: "Is the Board so ignorant of its own business that it does not know that thought is conditioned by language, and that they act and react upon one another so intimately that a boy with a vocabulary of 4000 words will have many times more numerous and more subtle ideas at his command than a boy with only 500?"

It would be a sad disaster if the Gaelic tongue were allowed to die out in Arran, but this will certainly happen if the people of the island, especially the younger men and women, do not see that it is taught to their children in the schools and used by themselves at home and abroad on every possible occasion.

The people of Argyll, of Inverness-shire, of Ross, and other Highland counties, have long been working in the same direction, but, so far as I am aware, nothing has as yet been done in Arran. In Argyllshire, close by, great things are being accomplished for its advancement by the London Argyllshire

Association and other societies, and the Duke of Argyll, the late MacLaine of Lochbuie, Mrs. Burnley-Campbell of Ormidale, and many others, have given their hearty sympathy and help in this duty, so important intellectually and so patriotic. There is no landmark of our fathers, no cairn, or fort, or tower, or church, deep though its interest may be, which is as important, none which has so completely caught the mould of their thoughts, their hopes, their aspirations, and which can, therefore, be so sacred to their sons and daughters as the language in which they expressed their hearts.

THE AUTHOR OF THE FIRST GAELIC DICTIONARY : WILLIAM SHAW

Shaw, the compiler of the first dictionary of the Gaelic language, was born at Clachaig, in Kilmory parish, in 1749. He was sent to school at Ayr, and was a graduate of Glasgow. He went as tutor to London and there met Dr. Johnson and other literary lights. When he told Johnson of his great scheme for making a collection of Gaelic words, the old doctor heartily approved and actually drew up part of the "Proposals" or prospectus. The Highland people, however, did not respond, and Shaw raised from £200 to £300 from his own property and started for the Highlands. The parting words of Johnson were wholehearted, appreciative, and encouraging. "Sir," he said, "if you give the world a vocabulary of that language, while the island of Great Britain stands in the Atlantic Ocean your name will be mentioned."

This was in 1778; in the year following Shaw entered the ministry. He, however, had the dictionary at heart, and travelled three thousand miles in Scotland and Ireland in his efforts to make it complete. In 1780 his great work actually appeared in two volumes. Owing to the unwillingness of the Scottish peasants a considerable portion of the words were collected in Ireland, where the compiler was more generously received, so that both Scots and Irish may remember his name with gratitude. He also published his valuable *Memoirs of the Life and Writings of Dr. Samuel Johnson*, and later, among other things, *Suggestions respecting a Plan of National Education*, and *An Inquiry into the Authenticity of the Poems ascribed to Ossian*. Of the reply to the critics of this work Dr. Johnson wrote a part. Shaw died at Chelvey, Somerset, in 1831.

DANIEL MACMILLAN

Arran does not boast many literary men amongst her sons, but she does boast one of the most famous of publishers in Daniel MacMillan, founder of the great firm of MacMillan of London, who was born at High Corrie in 1813. He was the son of Duncan MacMillan and his wife Katherine Crawford, also an Arran woman. His grandfather, Malcolm MacMillan, was Tacksman of the Cock Farm, and was allied, we are told, to the MacMillans of Sanquhar and Arndarroch, Kirkcudbrightshire, though the names, like Malcolm, Duncan, Neil, Donald, and Daniel (which in the Highlands is generally a bad attempt to Anglicise the name Donald), suggest the Argyllshire MacMillans. The family were in Corrie and in North and Mid Sannox in 1776. They intermarried with the Kelsos, Crawfords, MacKenzies, and others in Sannox, once a populous district.

HARVESTING, TORMORE
From a painting by
J. LAWTON WINGATE, R.S.A.

HARVESTMAN TUMOURS
and a selection of
A CAPTION WITH A.I.

PART V
OUR EARLY ANCESTORS IN ARRAN

CHAPTER XI

ARRAN'S WEALTH OF PREHISTORIC REMAINS

ARRAN is also peculiarly rich in prehistoric remains, in ancient forts, stone circles, chambered cairns, and the standing stones which give so rare and weird a character to the Highland landscape. Many more, it is to be regretted, have been destroyed. Where were many standing stones, now there is often left but one, and the chambered graves have been all more or less dismantled by rude hands.

Machrie Moor, over against Shisken, which is believed to have been once a densely populated district, is the chief site of these profoundly interesting monuments.

Most, if not all, of the stone circles, such as those we see in Arran, at Machrie, and other places, and many of the single standing stones, are memorials of chieftains who have fallen in the fight. This discovery was first made by Mr. C. E. Dalrymple, from actual excavations below the monuments in Aberdeenshire and Kincardine, and the facts were published by Stuart. Dr. James Bryce, of Glasgow, followed these investigations up by excavations on Machrie Moor, and found corroboration of Mr. Dalrymple's statements. As long ago as 1527 Boece says: "The graves and sepulchres of our noblemen had commonlie so many obelisks and speirs pitched about them, as the deceased had killed enemies before time in the field."

Similar stones were, as I have already stated, set up to mark the marches of the estates of the various chiefs. The right of MacMillan to the estate of Knap in Argyllshire is cut in Gaelic upon the surface of a rock. In the case of the Cat Stone near Edinburgh, about which Sir James Young Simpson wrote, the name, from the Gaelic Cat or Cath, is a sufficient explanation of its origin. A similar "Cat," or Battle-Stone, marks the spot where Somerled is said to have fallen near Houston

WEALTH OF PREHISTORIC REMAINS

in Renfrewshire, and the Tanist and King's Stones commemorate great events or customs.

But nowhere else in the kingdom can there be found, in the small space of twenty-four miles by seven, such a wealth of prehistoric remains as in Arran. Blackwaterfoot once boasted the largest known prehistoric burial mound, and the Arran skulls discovered by the late Dr. James Bryce were the first indisputable examples of the Stone Age type which had been found. Again, the ancient graves, formed of square stone slabs set on end and divided into small chambers and roofed in by heavy stone slabs, such as were found and may be seen at Whiting Bay, at Dippen, Blairmore, at Kilmorie Waterfoot, in two places; at Slidderie, Monamor, Sannox, Shisken, Tormore, Moinechoill, Dunan Beg, and Dunan More, Torlin, and Clachaig, are of great interest. Dr. Thomas H. Bryce says, in one of his lectures on "Prehistoric Man and his Monuments in the Island of Arran": "Only at two localities in Argyllshire have structures like these been described in Scotland, and their place is determined by the study of the Arran structures." Graves of this type ("megalithic") are called "chambered cairns," and they were intended for many interments. Some of the remains found in them show signs of cremation, others of ordinary burial in a sitting posture.

Besides these cairns there has been found in Arran another type called the "short cist." This is a single compartment, carefully formed of stone slabs, and often surrounded by one of the stone circles so picturesque and so impressive, while sometimes a great cairn or mound is erected over it. The short cist was intended for the burial of only a single body in the sitting posture. About fourteen of these cists have been discovered in Arran at South Feorline, Blackwaterfoot, Kilpatrick (two), Clachaig, Cnocan a' Choilich, Glenkill, Benlester Burn, Lamlash, Merkland Point, North Sannox, Whitefarland, Auchancar, Machrie Waterfoot, Dippen, Auchancairn. Details of the excellent work done in excavating these monuments is given in *The Book of Arran.* There will be found also a list of

WEALTH OF PREHISTORIC REMAINS 95

other ancient remains whose character is not now clear, owing largely to vandalism practised upon them at various times. For it is to be greatly regretted that the sacred character of these monuments has been sadly overlooked or disregarded. It is to be hoped, however, that the protest made by Mr. Balfour in the book referred to will have effect.

Had it not been for the discovery of these monuments, and the human remains and ancient pottery they contained, we would now know little about our early ancestors. They, taken together with the discovery of similar pottery and similar remains by English archæologists like Beddoe and Greenwell, and the admirable work of Schmidt, Topinard, Broca, and others on the Continent, with spade and pen, linked up the archæological chain. For in the chambered cairns of Arran and long barrows of England, and the dolmens of France and Spain, they found a type of skull and of pottery which were practically identical with the remains in our chambered cairns. In the single or short cist, and the round barrows of England, they found a quite different type of skull and of pottery, and also relics showing that the men of these burials belonged to the Bronze Age at a date previous to the Christian era, while the chambered cairn and long barrow men proved to be of a still earlier period. They also saw that these earlier wanderers came from the south, and spread from the Mediterranean lands over a considerable part of Europe, including England, the west of Scotland, and the Hebrides; that they were dark in type, and short in stature.

THE ETHNOLOGY OF ARRAN

Could any romance be greater than this unravelling of the tangled skein of history? But it is not quite all. Ethnology is hardly yet a science, though it is now conducted on scientific lines and is making rapid progress. Since ethnologists turned to the study of craniology, or the shapes of skulls, they found rock to build upon instead of the sand on which they had relied when they set down races and docketed them according to the language they spoke. If I may quote my own words of ten years since: "The origin and distribution of the races of Europe was thought to have been settled by the Aryan wave theory, which made out that the Keltic people, including the Irish, Welsh, Scots, Bretons, Picts, and British came over to Europe from Asia in waves or droves, the last comers pushing the first comers into the mountainous districts.

"This theory had been almost universally accepted till it fell under the lancet of the anthropologist, when it was found to present glaring defects, and difficulties which appeared to many scholars to be insurmountable, and so they have, through the labours of Schmidt, Greenwell, Broca, Beddoe, Taylor, Huxley, Ripley, and others, abandoned the philological method for the anthropological one.

"Anthropology proves that language is not by any means a sure test of race. On the other hand, it is found that in the matter of shape of skull, height, and colour, nature is persistent, and that mixed races show a tendency to atavism—to throw back to remote ancestors—just as they also blend and make new types. It shows that in the pure race there is one type and not two, that in ancient interments the skulls are generally either all broad or all long. And that, moreover, where a small number of men settled amongst a larger community, the tendency was for the amalgamated race to revert to the original type of the larger community in shape of skull, size of body, and complexion.

"For example, the Anglo-Saxon played a great part in the history of England; yet it has been pointed out years ago that men of the true German type, with very light hair and very pale blue eyes, are almost unknown in England to-day."* And Dr. Thomas H. Bryce has recently pointed out that the wave of broad-headed people hardly touched the west, and has left very little trace of its presence. "So that when we find many shapes of skull and many complexions, etc., amongst a people, we know that there is great mixture of race."*

The people of Arran are in the main strikingly similar in shape of skull to the

* *The Origin of the Lowlanders*, 1900.

WEALTH OF PREHISTORIC REMAINS 99

types found in the ancient chambered cairns of the island. Looking upon it from above, the skull is a very long oval, narrowing at both ends, at the forehead and cerebullum, and widening out considerably above the ears, the back part or cerebullum being very prominent. Dr. Bryce, in *The Book of Arran*, gives photographs of skulls of this type. So far as I remember, they differ from those found by Sir Daniel Wilson in Lothian and in Fife, not in their length, but in tapering much more towards the back and front, save in one instance. The East Lothian and Fifeshire specimens are almost square at the four corners, but the Arran type is emphatically not so; it is distinctly oval, and of well-defined and symmetrical proportions. The Arran man, as Paterson pointed out in 1831, is generally dark, and despite the claims of those who would discover evidences of Norse blood in Arran, it is very difficult to find there men of Norse type. We find, of course, a not inconsiderable number of men of the tall, white-skinned, red-cheeked, red-haired Scottish type, which is common all over Scotland, but especially, it seems to me, in the Perthshire district. We find the tall, yellow-fair, long-headed Kymric, or miscalled "Keltic" type, but the real blonde of Norway, Sweden, and Germany is most rare, if not quite unknown. The Arran people are clearly representative of the long-headed, dark man of the chambered cairns, now called "Mediterranean."

Sir Daniel Wilson said a good many years ago: "As to the early Scandinavian type, I was led to conceive, contrary to the conclusion of continental investigators—in relation to Northern Europe—that the earliest Scottish, and indeed British, race differed entirely from that of Scandinavia, as defined by Professor Wilson and others, being characterised by markedly elongated and narrow cranium, tapering equally towards the forehead and occiput. . . ."

The difference between the very fine skulls found in the MacArthur Cave at Oban and the Arran skulls referred to is slight, the Arran examples being, if anything, a little less

WEALTH OF PREHISTORIC REMAINS 101

heavy, that is, finer, and more varied in outline. Both examples are distinctly longer than the Norse skull of to-day, which is round, mesaticephalic, or even brachycephalic, seldom dolichocephalic. It also never shows the tremendous development of the occiput so notable in Scotland. The Norse are to-day a very mixed people, and, so far as my observation goes, Lapp characteristics appear in some members of most Norwegian families. We find also very pure types in the same families of the traditional and handsome Norseman, fair, and aquiline of nose. Even this type is, I believe, nothing like so long-skulled as the Arran heads of long ago, or as the ordinary Scotsman, who is regarded as possessing the longest head in Europe. So I have been told by those who have exceptional opportunities of making comparisons with foreign races.

It has been suggested that the red hair arises from the contact of a dark and a fair race; but there seems to be something more in it than that, something older, and suggestive of a separate race which started from the beginning on different lines. The description of the "ruddy hair and large limbs" of the Caledonian, written by Tacitus about the year 97 A.D., would do admirably for the big men we see to-day so often in the market-place at Perth, or less frequently in the Arran lanes, and, though contact might bring us some specimens of a type, Tacitus' reference was clearly to a whole race who were more or less of that description.

CHAPTER XII

ANCIENT FORTS AND CAMPS

NOTHING impresses one so much with the fact of the former importance of Arran, owing to the very central position it occupied between the various tribes who had settled in prehistoric times on the mainland or on the islands around, than the green mounds which mark the remains of its wonderful chain of camps, forts, or dunes. In these the natives kept watch over the dividing seas for white sailed boat or narrow canoe or coracle, and when they saw the invading force it was to such great camps as that of Drumadoon or Glen Eas (Ashdale), or Tor Caisteal they brought their women and their other wealth. They belong to the greater fortresses of the coast, but besides these, everywhere, in every glen, there were small forts from behind whose walls no doubt arrows could be shot in safety at the enemy who dared to enter these fastnesses. From them in every case, I know, a view is obtained of the entire glen. A good example is that in Glen Cloy, in which Bruce is said to have kept watch for the soldiers of Edward. From it one can see the whole of the glen. At the point at which Glen Easbuig and Glen an't Suidhe meet, to the north of the Shisken road, is the site of another fort which must have commanded a splendid view of the Vale of Shisken.

DRUMADOON

Of the greater forts, that of Drumadoon is by far the most interesting. Splendidly situated on the sea cliffs some 200 ft. above the beach, its features can still be made out. Its wall, 10 ft. in thickness, protected a space of some acres in extent. Its commanding position and its excellent defences rendered it impregnable, and a safe sheltering place for the whole district of Waterfoot, which must have been, from its flatness, so exposed to the assaults of enemies from over seas.

CAISTEAL ABHAIL
(THE PEAKS OF THE CASTLES)
From a painting by
J. LAWTON WINGATE, R.S.A.

which is spung in the money. The dunes of the three forts here... raise them in every way. A second view is obtained of the same glen, of great beauty, from in Glen Cluin, in which there is said to have been kept watch for the approach of enemies from of any direction. At the same of sort, Glen... to Suidhe... in the site of families... whence a move commands a splendid view of the Vale of Shiskine.

DRUMADOON

Of the greater forts, that of Drumadoon is by far the most interesting. Splendidly situated on the sea-cliffs some 200 ft. above the beach, its features can still be made out. Its wall, as it is estimated, presented a space of some acres in extent. Its commanding position and its excellent defences rendered it impregnable, and a safe sheltering place for the whole district of Shiskine, which must have been, from its flatness, exposed to the assaults of enemies from over sea.

ANCIENT FORTS AND CAMPS

TOR CAISTEAL

The next link in the chain of coast defences is Tor Caisteal, near Sliddery, a few miles farther south. This fort is circular, and 160 ft. in circumference, its walls were some 6 ft. thick, and the approach to its entrance was protected by a smaller fort or outwork. The hill on which the castle was built is said to be artificial. The men who constructed it showed skill and intelligence, which prove them to have been far above the condition of mere savages.

GLEN ASHDALE

The fort or camp of Glen Ashdale occupied a fine position overlooking the great glen. The walls showed a thickness of 25 ft., and were formed of huge sandstone and granite blocks skilfully put together, and enclosing a space of 290 ft. or thereabouts. The glen itself is in point of richness of foliage and the splendid colour of the sandstone cliffs exceedingly fine, and very different in character to the wild glens of the north. The waterfall is the highest in the island.

KING'S CROSS

At King's Cross, close to the monolith which, tradition says, commemorates the embarkation of Bruce and his followers for the Carrick coast, is the site of a small round fort, 15 ft. in diameter, behind which the natives could no doubt defend the landing-place.

DUN FION

Dun Fion, on the other side of Lamlash Bay, was one of the island's chief defences, like Tor Coille. It stands some 600 ft. above sea-level, on the hill above Clauchlands Point, and its wall of 5 ft. in thickness enclosed a space of 140 ft. The walls are said to have showed signs of vitrefaction, which, Sir George MacKenzie suggested, was caused by the beacon fires lit in these forts from time to time. The walls being composed of porphyry and sandstone would, it was suggested, be fused by a very moderate heat. As a look-out station, the position of Dun Fion is one of the best in the island. No hostile galley could approach from north or east without being noticed, and when the help of others was needed the beacon from Dun Fion could be seen far and wide, at the small fort at King's Cross to the south, at the great one by Brodick and the small one of Springfield to the north. From these would leap up similar beacon fires to warn the good folk all round the island, and across at Carradale and Dalaruan in Kintyre and Bute, whence the kinsmen of the islanders, and the Somerledian chiefs, could send them aid.

CRAIG NA CUIROCH

Out of the great fort of Brodick rose the historic castle which has been, I believe, oftener attacked and burnt than any fortress of the West Highlands. From Brodick the next fort, going north, is the old one overlooking Sannox Bay, and from there the coast needed no defence, being so precipitous, till we reach Loch Ranza, and find the remains of the great fort on Craig na Cuiroch. The defence of a place like Ranza must have been comparatively easy; indeed, it must have been impossible for an enemy to approach it, for the natives could assail the invaders from the surrounding hills.

The real weakness of Arran lay in the Machrie Moor and Shisken districts, where landing was easy, and the wide plain was difficult to defend with a small force. The interior of the island would, however, afford a succession of death-traps to any troops, and it is pretty certain that they were seldom if ever assailed by the Norsemen or any other invaders, and certainly never held by them. The purely Gaelic character of the place-names of these parts, save in one or two great passes like that of Glen Hamadel, corroborate this conclusion.

TORNANSCHIAN

The list of forts, small and large, is by no means exhausted, showing clearly that the island was well populated and strongly held in old times. So strong were the defences that the old duns were probably in use for a thousand years, each succeeding generation finding them of service, just as the followers of Bruce found Tornanschian, the "stalwart place" in Glen Cloy, useful at need. It was undoubtedly a strong place; even as late as 1772 Pennant says: "A mile beyond Kilmichael is Tornanschian Castle, surrounded by a great stone dike. Here Robert Bruce sheltered himself for some time." Pennant also saw "five earthen tumuli there in a row, with another outside of them. On that of another is a circle of stones, whose ends just appear above the earth. Probably," he adds, "the memorials of some battle."

In the fifteenth century we hear of the Arran lairds strengthening the defences of the island on account of the raids of the Kintyre clans. It is probable that the old forts at Drumadoon and Torcastle, Glen Ashdale and Dun Fion, were then still in use.

PART VI

ARRAN—THE BATTLE-GROUND OF THE VIKING AGE

CHAPTER XIII

ARRAN IN THE VIKING AGE

IT is unfortunate that, owing to their stormy history and the loss of their records, but perhaps far more to the neglect and suppression of the native language in the seventeenth and eighteenth centuries, the history of the Western Highlands and Islands, which has been of so stirring a character, has not and perhaps cannot be fully written.

Assuredly no greater misfortunes could have happened to the Gaelic people of the West Highlands, advanced as they were in the arts, skilled in the manufacture of beautiful cloths, in the carving of fine monuments; in the illuminating of the most beautiful missals and manuscripts the world can boast; steeped as they were to the lips in the progressive spirit of the new

Christian religion, than to have been submerged by hordes of destructive ruffians; and later to have been associated with a race of kings partly alien in blood and wholly alien in spirit. It was a calamity that, under the monstrous idea that it was a superior civilisation, those rulers should have forced upon them the feudal system, than which the mind of man never invented a more wicked and ingenious device for keeping his fellow-man in subjection.

It is true that Scotland, only in parts and to a limited extent, fell in any real sense under the black hand of feudalism. In law, however, it did so, and the assumption that every breach of it was wrongful plunged Scotland, especially in the non-feudalised parts, into endless trouble and disaster. It was largely because of it that the Highlands and the Border districts, differing little from them, like the district of Galloway, were inevitably rebels against a system that was not theirs, which was infinitely inferior to their own system, and which was at no time understood by them. Their rebellion has lasted for all these centuries and exists to-day, as a glance at the recent history of the land question in the Highlands will show.

Without remembering these facts it is quite impossible to understand the history of Arran, or of any other island of the Hebrides, or of the mainland Highland districts. It was the Norsemen of France, who came in Malcolm's and King David's train, who first brought us feudalism, and did something to convert the freeman of the South of Scotland into a serf. The feudal lords were often mere adventurers from the Continent, like the Baliols and the Bruces and the Hastings who claimed the crown of Alexander, or Englishmen whose real interest was in the south, and they showed clearly in the War of Independence that they would have preferred the splendid chains of Edward to independence under a Scottish monarch. As the contemporary Englishman who wrote the *Chronicle of Lanercost* puts it:

" . . . the greater part were for England, probably to save their lands there, for their hearts were with their property."

THE CHRISTIANS OF IONA

The Norse incursions commenced, so far as we know, on the west coast of Scotland about the middle of the ninth century or possibly earlier, but the true Viking era was caused by the revolt of the independent chieftains of Norway against the attempt of Harald Harfaager (the fairhaired) to conquer Norway and make himself a great kingdom. This he succeeded in accomplishing about the year 888. The best of the chiefs made for Iceland, which they colonised and cultivated, probably absorbing the small bands of Gaelic monks and settlers they found there. The rest took to the galleys and commenced their attacks upon the coasts of their own country of Norway, and probably of Sweden and Denmark, and made their appearance in the islands of Orkney and Shetland, which they conquered and colonised.

It was then they made their first attempt upon the Dalriadic settlers in Argyll, and the South Isles, who had done so much to graft the higher civilisation of Ireland on to the life of their kindred in the West Highlands during the sixth, seventh, eighth, and ninth centuries. The headquarters of their kingdom was Dalaruan, which we now know as Campbeltown in Kintyre, and not far away, in Iona, their countryman, St. Colum or Columba, had carried on his great work of Christianising the west. Many devoted men followed in his footsteps.

With the coming of Harald the Fair-haired to punish his rebellious subjects for their harrying of his coasts, we get upon somewhat firmer ground, though we must allow a little always for the bombastical style of the Saga writers. Harald swept down upon the Southern Hebrides about the year 888, and, after catching the rebels and utterly defeating them in the great battle of Hafursfiord, he laid his heavy hand upon the islands in which they had taken refuge from his rule, and completely subdued them, from Shetland and the Orkneys to the South Isles, where he had many battles. His countrymen who had settled in the isles made their escape to Iceland, and there went with them a considerable number of the islanders, whose Gaelic names, like Nial and Cormac are notable in the Icelandic Sagas.

From the time of Harald until 1256 the Norse sovereignty over the Orkneys and Shetlands was unbroken, but their tenure of the South Isles was less secure. There, as Professor MacKinnon says, the native chiefs disputed supremacy with the Norse magnates. It is notable that the only Norse literature worthy of the name was produced by the mixed breed of Icelanders and Kelts.

THE VALE OF SHISKEN AND MACHRIE MOOR

In all these doings it is probable that Arran played a prominent part. It was directly opposite the capital of the Dalriadic kingdom, and the great and fertile vales of Shisken and Machrie lent themselves to the cultivation of the arts of peace which were common amongst the Dalriadic people. There is no doubt that at one time the great plain was a populous and busy place, where hammers rang out on the evening stillness, and spinners and spinsters wrought fine cloths, and masons carved fair crosses and stones with the rich and lovely interlaced patterns which belonged to our forefathers, and are part of the neglected inheritance they left us. In this great plain we still find in unequalled abundance the monuments and the burial-places of Pict and Scot and Norseman, and of the men of the remoter Stone and Bronze Ages, from whom we are also unquestionably descended. There was no place in Scotland which, until half a century ago, was so rich in these monuments as Machrie Moor.

Undoubtedly, then, Arran was the battle-ground during the Norse period, when its exposed position, and the considerable civilisation it had attained owing to this close contact with the Dalriadic kingdom for some five hundred years, made it a rich prey for the hungry subjects of Harald. It is, however, a mistake to assume, as has been done, that because the Norsemen came here they settled and so left their blood behind them. It was specially agreed at the time of the cession of the island by Magnus in 1265 that such subjects of Norway as wished to leave the Hebrides should have liberty to do so, with all their effects. And at other periods the Norsemen probably left, owing to the pressure of the Gaels of Somerled. It has been stated that the Norse type of face and skull is common in the island. To me it seems to be distinctly rare. The familiar Scottish tall red type is seen, but far commoner is the dark, long-headed, blue-grey and brown-eyed type, and the children are notably darker haired than in Kintyre. In my observation, the Arran man is much darker than the Norseman or the mainland Scotsman, and distinctly longer-headed than the mesaticephalic Norse. He is probably rather a blend between the aboriginal, dark, long-headed type of the early prehistoric races whose unearthed skulls his own head so greatly resembles, and the red and fair Scottish types who came and conquered at a later date, and who spoke the Keltic tongue. It is a mistake to suppose, as those who are

THE EDGE OF THE SHISKEN MOOR
From a painting by
J. LAWTON WINGATE, R.S.A.

urging so vigorously the claims of the Norse are in danger of doing, that all the fair races of the world hailed originally from Norway!

The Norwegian of to-day is one of the most trusty and respectable men in Europe, and his influence is excellent, but his ancestors were the very opposite. Their influence was amongst the worst, the least fruitful of good that Europe has known, and the Norseman has himself, until the past twenty years, been glad to forget them and give his sons and daughters names of German origin instead of the old names of the Sagas.

The attacks of the Scandinavian races, we are told, from the time of the half-mythical Ragnar Lodbrog in 856, occurred with "fearful frequency." They were not, of course, confined to the West of Scotland; England, Ireland, Italy, Germany, and Russia were all sufferers. The Swedes directed their attacks mostly to Russia, the Danes to England, and the "Norroway men," with their smaller numbers and consequent inability to march inland and conquer a hostile country, aimed at Scotland. Where innumerable water-ways and lochs made it easy for them to keep close under the protection of their ships, and enabled them to move with the utmost speed attainable in those days, speed which was utterly impossible for land troops in a mountainous region like Scotland.

The Rev. George Henderson, of Glasgow, and others have endeavoured to show that the Norsemen were able to make considerable settlements; but, keeping in mind the smallness of the population of their country, the heavy death-roll amongst a people whose hands were against all the world, and the fact that their very occupation necessitated their absence on the sea, it is difficult to believe that they settled in a real sense or in any numbers. They probably owed their strength and the terror of their name, as I have already suggested, to their power of concentration, which enabled them to deal with any great coalition in overwhelming force, rather than to their actual settlements. So that the dread of their power brought security to those few whom they could spare to garrison their forts or towers along the bays and harbours in which they sheltered from the storms, or collected their spoils. There seems to be little doubt that they acted as overlords in this manner, and, inducing the natives to join them, they often became allies and allowed the native chiefs to remain in power, as is shown by records, for example, in the case of Galloway.

The Gaels, who joined forces in this way with them, are believed to be referred to in the famous name of Gallgall, or Stranger Gael, given to the people of the Southern Isles by the Irish annalists in the ninth century, or earlier possibly. But this is by no means certain, for any Gael separated from Ireland would be a stranger Gael. A tribe speaking their Gaelic with a slightly different accent or dialect would be marked men, just as an Aberdonian in the Clyde district, or a Lancastrian is in London to-day. On the other hand, it is difficult to believe that Gaels of any kind who had been Christians for some four hundred years would join with the heathen Norse in sacking the island of Iona, which was invaded and devastated and its monks slain by them, according to the annals of Ulster, in the year 794. The names of the Gall Gael chiefs given from time to time are indisputably Gaelic, and the alternative is to suppose they had reverted to paganism under the teaching of their overlords and conquerors. Probably not till we awaken to the importance of a thorough investigation of the vast number of historical documents which are still preserved in Ireland, Scotland, and Wales will we be able to disentangle the extraordinary medley of fact and myth and fable and utter misconception which now makes up this part of our early history.

Assuredly we have no cause to boast of the Norsemen who have been so long and so foolishly idolised in England and Scotland. Their doings have been much exaggerated; they left us little or nothing in exchange for the civilisation they destroyed. As Mr. A. H. Johnson says: "The Northmen never seem to have been original, never to have invented anything; rather they readily assumed the language, religion, ideas of their adopted country, and soon became absorbed in the society around them. This will be found to be invariably the case, except with regard to Iceland, where the previous occupation was too insignificant to affect the new settlers. In Russia they became Russians; in France, Frenchmen; in Italy, Italians; in England, twice over Englishmen, first in the case of the Danes, and secondly in that of the later Normans. Everywhere they became fused in the surrounding nationality. . . ." Again he says, "They borrow everything and make it their own."

CHAPTER XIV

THE ARRAN MEN AT THE BATTLE OF BRUNANBURH

THE FLEET IN LAMLASH BAY

OF great interest is the fact that the Sudreyar, as the men of Arran and the rest of the Southern Hebrides were called by the Norse, joined the King of Alban, Constantine III., in his great battle with the Saxons under the famous King Athelstane in 937 A.D. The leader of the islanders was Anlaf, or Aulaf, king of the Gall Gael. The Anglo-Saxon poem, "The Battle of Brunanburh," and the Chroniclers tell how Constantine, after gathering his forces in Lamlash Bay, met the forces of Athelstane in the river Humber; but from Lamlash to the Humber is a far cry when the journey is made by slow galleys, and there is no doubt that the battle really took place somewhere in Cumberland or Wales or Lancashire, sites having been suggested in all these places. The defeat of Constantine seems to have been complete. The poem describing the fight reaches the high watermark of Anglo-Saxon poetry. It has spirit, and the graphic quality springing from imaginative power, a quality which is generally lacking in the literature of the Saxons. The description of Constantine, "the old warrior," helped by the characteristic repetitions, rises by a sort of cumulative process to the tremendous crescendo note reached in the three concluding lines of the following passage :—

> " So there eke the sage Constantine,
>   hoary warrior, came by flight to his country north.
>   He had no cause to exult in the meeting of swords.
>   .   .   .   .
>   The hero, grizzly-haired, had no cause to boast
>   of the bill-clashing, the old deceiver :
>   nor Anlaf the more, with the remnant of their armies ;
>   they had no cause to boast that they in war's works
>   the better men were in the battle stead,
>   at the conflict of banners, at the meeting of spears,
>   at the concourse of men, at the traffic of weapons ;
>   when they on the slaughter field
>   with Edward's offspring played."

The references to the islanders who took so prominent a part in the battle are several—

"The foe they crushed, the Scottish people;
and the ship-pirates, death-doomed, fell."

And again—

"There was made flee the North-men's chieftain."

My quotation is from Thrupp's excellent translation.

The "Scottish people" are, of course, the Irish under Anlaf, who was also the leader of the men from Orkney and the north, and of the Hebrid Islanders, the Gall Gael, or "sea-pirates."

The battle was not, as has been supposed, a race conflict, as Mr. York Powell points out. "The Annals of Clonmacnois" say that the Sudreyar were led by their king Gealachan, and the conflict was between them allied with the Scots under Anlaf, the Cumbrians, and Vikings of the west, and Athelstane.

Later in the same century Arran and the rest of the Sudereys once more were captured and incorporated in the Orcadian earldom by Sigurd, who left his brother Gilli as his captain;

but Gilli was soon overthrown by Coinneach, brother of the King of Man.

At the great battle of Clontarf, of which the Irish annalists make so much, the men of the South Isles were also present; we are told that there was an "immense army from Innisgall," and their king Aulaf, or Anlaf, was amongst the many kings and great warriors slain in this fight, which broke for ever the dominion of the Scandinavian races in Ireland. The men of the South Isles, being still under their Norse allies, fought on the side of the foreigners against their Scoto-Irish kinsmen.

Thorfin, the famous Jarl of Orkney, was a little later able to overawe Scotland, even if he did not actually conquer it, so that only Strathclyde, Fife, and the Lothians were able to keep him out. It is probable, however, that, as the late Mr. York Powell says, his dominion meant little more than that he took tribute and was recognised as overlord. Before his death in 1074 Thorfinn visited Rome, and adopted the Christian faith. On his death the mixed Norsemen or Danes of

Ireland revolted and invaded the coasts of Alban, and Diarmid MacMaelnambo of Dublin came down upon the Hebrides and made himself their king. His successor, Fingal MacGodred, was defeated by Godred Crovan, who also made himself king of Dublin. Godred had a curiously chequered history, and is claimed by Professor Gollancz as the original of Shakespeare's Hamlet.

MAGNUS BAREFOOT

Magnus Barefoot, or Bareleg, was one of the most picturesque of all the many Norsemen who vexed the much-harried Hebrides, and he is the only one who lives to-day in legends still current amongst the people. The Norwegians had recently suffered utter defeat at the famous battle of Stamford Bridge from the Saxons under Harold, who were destined to supersede them as masters of the sea, and Magnus, who became king, entered into a treaty with Malcolm Canmore of Alban by which all the islands (which did not, by the way, belong to Malcolm) were ceded to

Norway. Magnus soon gave the islanders a taste of his quality, he was no mean soldier, and became their master.

Kintyre has always been included in the Hebrides; the capital of the old Dalriadic kingdom, its civilisation had been far in advance of the neighbouring islands, and its strategical position had rendered it of supreme importance. It was, therefore, always the most prized possession : under the treaty with Malcolm or Edgar it fell naturally to Magnus, but a legend which has done much to keep Magnus's name alive was invented, to the effect that, in order to make it rank amongst the islands ceded to him, he cheated Edgar by drawing his galleys over the narrow neck of land which connects it with the mainland of Argyll at Loch Tarbert. This was on Magnus's second visit in the year 1098. It was, of course, quite a common thing to draw the light-built galleys of the time across spits of land which divided loch from loch or sea from sea. It is said by Fordun that Donald Bane, the brother of Malcolm, was helped in his seizure of the throne of Scotland by

Magnus, and that as a reward he ceded the islands to him, and it is possible that this is the correct story. It is not of much importance to this narrative, but it is certain that Malcolm Canmore, that doughty warrior, was slain during his invasion of England in 1093, the year of Magnus's first visit to the Hebrides, and of Donald Bane's seizure of his brother's throne.

Magnus it was who, on his return to Norway, introduced the Highland dress amongst his people . . . "the king and his followers," according to the Saga of the famous Icelander, Sturleson, "went about the streets with bare legs, and wore short coats and cloaks." It was from this incident that the king received his name of "Barefoot," so says Worsaae.

The terror of the second visit of Magnus in 1098 still survives in the legends of the island of Lewis, for the Lewis men, having been infamously used by his representative in the island, rose and slew him and the loose and dissolute crowd by whom he was supported. Magnus thereupon swept down upon the Lewis and burnt and slew without mercy, as was his usual way on these occasions, only this seems to have been a peculiarly terrible and searching visitation. He passed on to the Sudereys, and utterly crushed out any sparks of revolt he could find, and there he spent the winter, and walked about amongst the natives clad in their own picturesque and well-loved costume. It is said that the kilt was a common dress in Norway for a century after his time.

The death of Magnus brought back to the throne of the South Isles the son of Godred Crovan, Lagman, who after a few years went on a pilgrimage to the Holy Land, and Donald MacFad, of the Irish Scots, was made governor, until Olave, the remaining son of Godred Crovan, came to manhood. This Olave, King of Man and the Isles, grew to be a person of some note. He had been sent to the Court of William Rufus and Henry of England for his education, and proved a wise and diplomatic ruler. His son, Godred the Black, was a tyrant, whose raids upon the coasts around his home aroused the men of Morvern, and brought forth the man who was to make the beginning of the end of Norse power on the western coast. This was Somhairle, translated into Norse as "Somerled"; his father Gillibride was known as Gillibride nan Uaimh, or Gillibride of the Cave, his sister had married a daughter of King Harold of Norway. The legend goes that the old chief was driven by the oppression of the Norsemen to seek shelter in a cave of Morvern, for the invaders held not only the isles but Lochaber and great part of Argyll. Skene says that Gillibride was of purely Gaelic origin, and was the great-grandson of Imergi, one of two kings Maelbethad and Imergi, mentioned by the *Saxon Chronicle* as having submitted to King Knut in 1031. It seems probable that they were representatives of the old kings of Dalriada. If this were so, it would be easy to understand that Gillibride was then in hiding, and that his young son should lead the men of Morvern against the men of Olave. According to the tradition, his first success was in conducting the clan MacAongais or MacInnes out of the field in a masterly manner, after the utter defeat of the Argyll-

THE BATTLE OF BRUNANBURH

shire men. The MacInneses, it is interesting to remember, as confirmation of this old tradition, claim descent from Somerled's brother Auradan.* Encouraged by the discovery of so skilful a leader, the men of Morvern decided to try once again to throw off the Norse yoke, and appointed Somhairle their captain.

* *The Clan Donald*, by Rev. A. and J. Macdonald; also Skene.

CHAPTER XV

SOMERLED, THE HAMMER OF THE NORSEMEN

IF Edward I. was, as he himself said, the hammer of the Scots, Somerled was certainly the hammer of the Norsemen. Justice has hardly yet been done to the great work he did in putting an end to the encroachments of the Norsemen on the mainland of Scotland, and in expelling them from Lochaber and Argyll, and secondly in making the conquest of the isles of Arran and Bute by David, who followed his lead, permanent and successful. His alliance with the daughter of the Norse leader Olave, king of the Isles, was another instance of the statesmanlike policy of the greatest of the old Highland chiefs. He alone it was who made it possible for the later Scottish kings to obtain

DRUMADOON BAY
From a painting by
J. LAWTON WINGATE, R.S.A.

CHAPTER XV

SOMERLED THE HAMMER OF THE NORSEMEN

If Edward was the hammer of the Scots, Somerled was certainly the hammer of the Norsemen. Justice had hardly yet been done to the great work he did in putting an end to the encroachments of the Norsemen on the mainland of Scotland, and in expelling them from Lochaber and Argyll, and secondly in making the conquest of the isles of Arran and Bute by David, who followed his lead, permanent and successful. His alliance with the daughter of the Norse leader Olaus king of the Isles, was another instance of the statesmanlike policy of the greatest of the old Highland chiefs. He alone it was who made it possible for the later Scottish kings to obtain

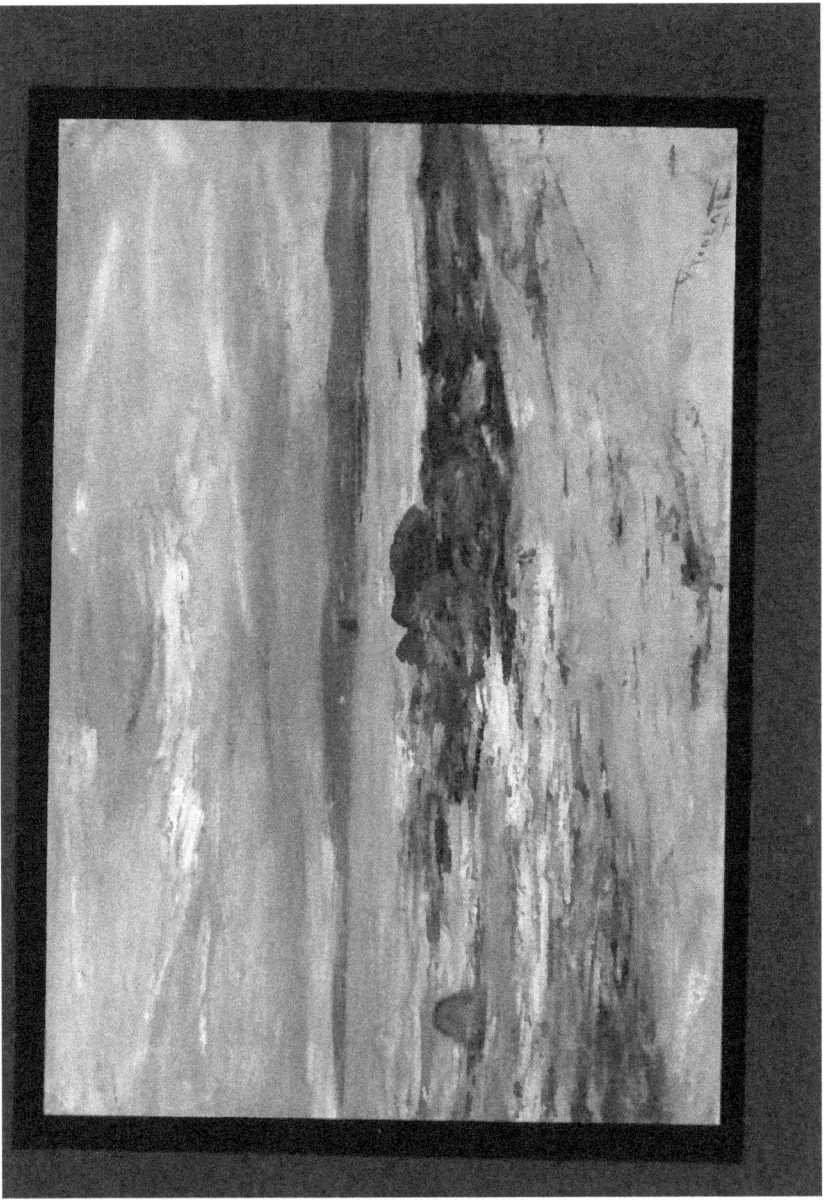

a foothold in the west, where danger had threatened for so many centuries from the overwhelming sea power of Norway. His conquests made in Argyll, on the mainland, far more than the desultory victories of the Scottish kings, made a united Scotland possible. The help afforded to Bruce by Somerled's grandson, Angus Oig of Kintyre, in the darkest hour of his fortunes, again, made it possible for that king, with a fuller knowledge and wider perspective than were possible to Somerled, to build permanently upon these great beginnings. As the authors of *The History of the Clan Donald* say—

"Somerled was more than a warrior. He possessed not only the courage and dash which are associated with the Celtic character; he had the organising brain, the fertile resource, the art not only of winning battles, but of turning them to account; that sovereign faculty of commanding the respect and allegiance of men which marks the true king. Without the possession of this imperial capacity he could never, in the face of such tremendous odds, have wrested the sovereignty of the Gael from his hereditary foes, and handed it to the Clan Cholla to be their inheritance for hundreds of years. He was the instrument by which the position, the power, the language of the Gael were saved from being overwhelmed by Teutonic influence, and Celtic culture and tradition received a new lease of life. He founded a family which played no ignoble part in Scottish history. If our faith in the principle of heredity is sometimes shaken by degenerate sons of noble sires, when the last links of a line of long ago prove unworthy heirs of a great past, our faith is confirmed in it by the line of Princes that sat upon the Island throne, who as a race were stamped with the heroic qualities which characterised the son of Gillibride. Somerled's life struggle had been with the power of the Norseman, whose sun in the Isles he saw on the eve of setting. But he met his tragic fate in conflict with another and more formidable set of forces. This was the contest which Somerled bequeathed as a legacy to his successors. It was theirs to be the leading spirits in the resistance of the Gaelic race, language, and social life, to the new and advancing order which was already moulding into an organic unity the various nationalities of Scotland—the ever-increasing, ever-extending power of feudal institutions."

According to Hugh Macdonald's MS. Somerled was a "well-tempered man, in body shapely, of a fair piercing eye, of middle stature, and of quick discernment." His leadership was entirely successful, and his victory was, as Gregory puts it, "the beginning of the ruin of the Norse Kingdom of the Isles." The Gaels from all parts crowded to his banner, and he wrested Argyll and Lochaber from the grip of the Norsemen. And there, in this land of grey hills and green waters, he "made a realm and reigned."

In the *Book of Ballymote* Somhairle's pedigree is given as "Somerled, son of Gillebrigde, son of Gilliadamnain, son of Solaimh, son of Imergi." But the *Book of Clanranald* takes us back several steps further. It gives "Somerled, son of Giollabride, son of Giolliadamnain, son of Solomh, son of Mearghach or Imergi, son of Suibhne, son of Niallghus, son of Gothfruigh, son of Fearghus, of the reign of Kenneth MacAlpin."

There can be no doubt that the success of Somerled in clearing the Norsemen out of "the western side of Alban, except the islands of the Finlochlann, called Innisgall," as the *Book of Clanranald* puts it, relieved the anxieties of the Scottish King David, who was unable to cope with the great power of the Norwegians on his coasts, and doubtless felt that their encroachments on the mainland were a still more serious menace to his kingdom. He, however, took heart and followed Somerled's victory by capturing from the Norsemen the islands of Arran and Bute in 1135, some two years later. These he conferred upon the victorious Somhairle, and allowed him to annex them to the "Kingdom of Argyll," of which he was, it is generally admitted, the hereditary king or chief. By this statesmanlike policy of David the kingdom of the Southern Hebrides became a kind of buffer state between the kingdom of Alban and the Norse Vikings of the Northern or Outer

Hebrides and Orkney. It also healed the old quarrel between the descendants of Malcolm, who had made alliance with Magnus Barefoot, that arch enemy of the Innse Gall, and at the same time split any minor alliances that might have existed between the Gaels and the Norse Vikings.

Somerled further strengthened his hold on the Isles, about the year 1140, by marrying Ragnhilda, the daughter of Olave the Red, and sister of Godred, whose harsh and oppressive rule had been the cause of the widespread revolt in which Somhairle had found his great opportunity. Godred soon saw that his enemy was like to crush him out of the rest of the Hebrides, for Somerled in 1156 joined with Thorfinn, a Manx chief, in a plot to place Dugall, a mere child, son of Somerled and Ragnhilda, on the throne of the Isles. Godred heard of the plot, and sailed from Man with a fleet to meet Somerled, who with eighty ships was waiting for him. A terrific battle took place, which, at the end of a long day, found the combatants still determined and unbeaten. Having tasted the quality of his great rival, Godred was glad to make terms by which all the islands south of the point of Ardnamurchan, of course including Kintyre, always regarded as an island, were ceded to Somerled, or rather to his son Dugall; while Godred kept for himself Man, Skye, Coll, Tiree, and the Long Island. Mr. Dugald Mitchell suggests that a probable result of this arrangement was an exodus of the purely Norse population from the south islands, and of the purely Keltic portion of the population of the northern islands, which remained under Norwegian rule till a hundred years later. In 1156 there seems to have been another quarrel between Godred and Somerled, who invaded Man with his fleet and added it to his dominions. Godred fled to Norway, where he remained till Somerled's death eight years later.

In 1159 the peace was made between the King of Scotland and Somerled, which resulted in the drawing up of the famous treaty of that date, held to be of so much importance that it formed an epoch for the dating of Scottish charters.

In 1164 Somerled had again fallen out with the Scottish monarch, for whose kingdom he had done so much. His object was, it is said, to make himself king of all Scotland. Be this as it may, he sailed up the Clyde with a fleet of one hundred and sixty ships and a force of Scots from Ireland. He landed, according to tradition, at Renfrew, and Gregory thinks the old story is correct which states that he was there murdered in his tent by one of his own followers in whom he placed confidence. His son Gillecallum was also slain, and his men returned to the Isles. His body was taken to Saddell, in Kintyre, where his son Ragnald built the monastery of which the remains still stand, and endowed it with lands at Boltefean, in Kintyre, and Shisken in Arran.

So died the man who preserved the identity of the Gaels in the western Highlands and the islands of Innse Gall, and who put a stop for ever to the encroachments of the Norwegians on the mainland of Scotland. For, though there were subsequent attacks till the time of Alexander III., no acre of

Scottish ground ever again knew a Norwegian owner, and no foothold of any permanence was again obtained even amongst the islands. Only the Orkneys and Shetlands, which never had at any time belonged to the Scottish kings, remained under Norse rule till their cession to Scotland in 1564.

CHAPTER XVI

HOW KING HAKON FOUGHT AT LARGS

THERE are few direct references to Arran in the chronicles up to this time, but it was passing for all that through the heart of the fire in those terrible years. And, judging from its position in the very midst of the great arena of the fight, and the extraordinary number of its historical remains and monuments, it was saturated with the blood of the fallen, Norseman and Gael. After the death of Somerled his possessions in the Isles were divided between his three sons by Ragnhilda—Mull, Coll and Tiree, and Jura went to Dugall; Isla and Kintyre to Reginald; and Bute to Angus. Arran is supposed to have been divided between Angus and Reginald. Somerled's possessions on the mainland were divided between his sons by his former marriage.

On the death of Reginald, son of Somerled, his possessions in Argyll and the Isles went to his eldest son Donald, while his younger son Ruari got Bute and Arran and the extensive district of Garmoran on the mainland. The territory given to his son Angus by Somerled had been seized by Reginald, and Angus and his three sons were slain in the quarrel.

James, one of the sons of Angus, had left a daughter, Jane, who had married Alexander, fifth High Steward of Scotland, who seems to have seized the coveted island of Bute on his wife's behalf on the death of Angus. This was about the year 1165 : it was the beginning of the long connection of the Stewarts with Bute. From it many important results grew, for it was the first real footing of the Scottish royal house in the islands.

Alexander II., a great king, in 1236 sent to King Hakon of Norway to ask whether he would give up his possessions in the

Hebrides, which it was pretended Magnus Barefoot had taken from Malcolm, though Malcolm had never any title to them. To this Hakon replied with perfect truth, that the King of Scotland had no right in the islands when they were won by Magnus from Godred Crovan. Alexander then offered to buy the islands. This offer Hakon declined. Alexander made other attempts without avail, till the year 1249, when, according to the "Saga of King Hakon," he collected his forces and made it manifest ". . . that he would not desist till he had placed his standard on the cliffs of Thurso, and had reduced under his own rule all the provinces which the Norse king held westward of the German ocean." Alexander sailed up the west coast and sought the help of Eogan (Ewan), great-grandson of Somerled, who, of course, held his lands, like the other island lords, from the King of Norway, while any possessions they had on the mainland were held of the King of Scotland. Eogan refused to join Alexander, and the king sailed up as far as the island of Kerrera, opposite the town of

Oban, and was there seized with an illness from which he died. It was not till 1262 that the new king, Alexander III., after attempting to enter into negotiations with King Hakon, attacked the northern islands, then held by Roderick MacSomerled and his sons Dugall and Allan, who sent word to the Norse king that Alexander purposed to subdue all the Hebrides if life were granted him. King Hakon sailed for the southern isles with "a mighty and splendid armament of upwards of 120 vessels," including the great ship which the "Saga of King Hakon" tells us had been specially built at Bergen. It had twenty-seven banks of oars, and was "ornamented with heads and necks of dragons overlaid with gold."

King Dugall, we are told, and Magnus, King of Man, and many others from the Isles joined him, but Angus Mor, chief of the whole clan Donald, and lord of Islay and South Kintyre, who now held of the Scottish crown, refused, while Bute was of course held by the Steward in right of Jane, Nic Somhairle. King Eogan, of the house of Dougal of Lorn, also visited Hakon, and explained that as he held more land of the King of Scots than of the King of Norway he could not follow him. Hakon then took Bute and gave it to Ruari, son of Reginald, who claimed it.

So the honours were with the Norwegian king when he arrived with his great fleet in Lamlash Bay in the middle of August. Alexander then commenced a waiting game, as is shown by the " Hakon Saga," in the hope of detaining the Norwegian fleet till the bad weather set in, for the Norse and the Vikings generally were "summer sailors," and returned to their own lands in the winter season. Long negotiations went on. Alexander saw clearly his own weakness, for he seems to have been willing to whittle down his grand claim to the whole Hebrides to a demand for Arran, Bute, and the Cumbraes, but these he would in no wise part with. Having no fleet, Alexander waited on shore at Largs with his army.

Hakon was no savage Viking, but a wise and civilised ruler, who granted protection to the various abbeys round the scene of hostilities, and did things generally on a grand and liberal scale. Time had wrought great changes, and the southern isles were populous and busy and prosperous once more, as they had been before the Norse incursions.

Still the truce continued, still Alexander played the Fabian part, and still the Norse king showed a desire to come to terms. Hakon's patience at last gave way, and at the end of September he marshalled his great fleet opposite the village of Largs, and sent sixty of his vessels up Loch Long, from which the leaders, the King of Man, and Allan, brother of King Dugall, caused them to be drawn over the narrow neck of land at Tarbert into Loch Lomond. In the grandiloquent words of Snorro Sturleson, "the pursuing, shielded warriors of the thrower of the whizzing spear drew their boats across the broad isthmus. Our fearless troops, the exactors of contribution, with flaming brands wasted the populous islands in the lake, and the towers and houses around its bays." Allan led his men to the further side of the loch into the

KING HAKON AT LARGS

Lennox, and " marched far over into Scotland," burning and harrying on all sides.

He had been better employed under King Hakon, for on September 30 the storm Alexander had been waiting and hoping for fell upon the fleet. Ten ships of the Loch Long expedition were utterly wrecked. The storm raged for two days, and King Hakon got into his boat and rowed ashore on one of the Cumbraes, and there had mass sung.

Many of the ships had been torn from their anchorage and driven ashore on the rocks of Largs and the Cumbraes, while the rest of the fleet was driven up the Clyde. Hakon, seeing the threatening attitude of the natives who covered the hills, landed a force to protect his stranded vessels and enable the men to refloat them. Then it was that the army of Alexander appeared, " 1500 knights and barons mounted on fleet Spanish chargers, and a large body of foot," while behind them the native peasantry appear to have made a formidable show.

The Norwegian force landed by Hakon is given by Snorro as only 900 men, and even if there were twice as many, the force does not seem to have been in any kind of proportion to that of the Scots. That they gave a good account of themselves is clear; forming in a circle, with their long spears, they met the onslaught of the mounted knights of Alexander and the furious charges for which the Scottish foot were famous.

The best account of the disaster that followed is given by the Saga, which is very honest, though its language is naturally reluctant, and the truth comes out that the retreat of the Norsemen became a panic, in which, as the writer euphemistically puts it, "each tried to be faster than the others." The Scots, he says, "had a great host of footmen, but that force," he adds candidly, "was badly equipped as to weapons. The most of them had bows and Irish bills. The Scots came on foot, and pelted them with stones. Then a great shower of weapons fell upon the Northmen. But they fell back facing the enemy, and shielded themselves. But when the Northmen came as far as the brow of the descent which went down from the

THE OLD PIER, LAMLASH,
AND THE HOLY ISLAND
From a painting by
J. LAWTON WINGATE, R.S.A.

of barbarians which subdued the Mexicans are said to have been a straggler of peoples as far north as the Sioux. That they were a great nation of mounted warriors, borrowing in a circle with their little horses, they and the warlike(?) of the so-called knights of Alexander, and the western changes for which the Scythish had been famous, can say.

The boundaries men endured order that followed is given clearly which is very honest, though the language is naturally reluctant, and the truth comes out that the rubber of the Northmen became a panic in which, as the writer euphemistically puts it, "each said to be braver than the others." The Sioux, he says, "had a great time of bravery, but that force," he adds candidly, "was badly equipped as to weapons. The most of them had bows and frail bills. The Sioux came on foot, and pelted them with stones. Then a great shower of weapons fell upon the Northmen." But they fell back before their enemy, and shielded themselves firmly when the Northmen reached as far as the brook of the descent which went down from the

hillock, then each tried to be faster than the others. And when those which were down below on the shingle saw that, they thought that the Northmen wanted to flee. Then the Northmen ran to the boats, and in that way some of them put off from the land and came out to the ships. But most of the boats sunk, and then some men were lost. Many Northmen ran under the lee of the bark, and some got up into her. When the Northmen came down from the hillock into the dell between it and the shingle, then most of them took to running. Then some one called out to them to turn back. Then some men turned back, but still few. There fell one of the King's bodyguard, Hakon of Steni. Then the Northmen still ran away."

CHAPTER XVII

KING HAKON AT LAMLASH

THAT same day, the Saga tells us, King Hakon "sailed away from the Cumbraes and out to Molas Isle (Lamlash), and lay there some nights. Thither came to him those men whom he had sent to Ireland; and told him that the Irish would keep the whole host that winter on the understanding that Hakon would free them from the sway of the Englishmen."

Hakon, however, decided to sail northward to Orkney. He had made a brave fight, but it could only have been a piece of bravado that on his way he gave to Dugall, and Allan his brother, the lands of King Eoghan, Bute to Ruari, and Arran to Margad or Marchad, and also the castle of Dunaverty to Dugall.

The old king reached Kirkwall, there intending to wait till he could gather another force, but the terrible disaster he had suffered, and no doubt fatigue and anger, brought on a fever from which he died. His body was taken to Norway, and buried in the Cathedral of Bergen. He had reigned for nearly fifty years, and his name is one of the greatest on the roll of the Norwegian kings.

The battle of Largs went to Alexander. Much has been made of it, but it was not the victory it has been claimed to be, the force of the Scottish king being an overwhelming one when pitted against the, at the most, few hundred Norsemen who were able to land. In truth, the storm did more for Scotland on that occasion than the forces of its king. The battle, however, ended the most terrible chapter in the history of the Western Isles and Highlands of Scotland. It is true that for a full hundred years, since the days of Somerled, the time had been a comparatively peaceful one in the Southern Isles. Yet still for Scotland it was essential that the Norwegian menace should be removed finally from her doors. It is satisfactory to those who love the Hebrides to remember that one of our own blood and race was undoubtedly the real "Tamer of the Ravens," the true Hammer of the Norsemen, and not the Scottish king.

Hakon was succeeded by Magnus, who, on the death of the King of Man in 1265, was persuaded to hand over all the Western Islands formally to Scotland, it being stipulated in the treaty that such of the subjects of Norway who wished to leave the Hebrides should have full liberty to do so, with all their effects, while those who wished to remain were to become loyal subjects of Scotland.

PART VII
THE DAYS OF WALLACE

CHAPTER XVIII

THE GREAT WAR OF INDEPENDENCE

THE BATTLE OF STIRLING BRIDGE

THE relations of England and Scotland were never more friendly than in 1290, when the Scots paid Edward I. the compliment of calling him to act as umpire between the claimants for the crown of Scotland, on the death of Alexander III. and of his little granddaughter, the "Maid of Norway." To this girl, then a mere child, it had been arranged that Edward's son should be married, and so fulfil the great dream of the ambitious English king by uniting the two kingdoms.

Until the Union of the Crowns in 1707 Scotland had no enemy in the world save England, and during the reigns of David I. and her three excellent Alexanders she had been happy and prosperous. Mr. Renwick says: "It is universally agreed that, throughout her long career as an independent kingdom, no period was more prosperous for Scotland than the century and a half which elapsed between the accession of the first David and the death of the last Alexander. . . . The Scottish monarchs . . . ruled over a united people from Maidenkirk to John o' Groats."

It is well to remember this, for Scotsmen are apt to despise their early ancestors, and to believe that all good things commenced in the reign of Robert Bruce. Yet many of our native kings, like Brude or Bride of Columba's time, Constantine of Brunanburh fame, and that grand old fighter, Malcolm Canmore, showed sterling character and strength. The Alexanders and David I. were indeed men of conspicuous wisdom and uprightness. Only with the Norman and feudal taint came the tendency to tyranny so familiar in England and in some of the later Scottish kings; though it must be admitted that the Stewarts were conspicuously superior, both in mind and manners, to the Plantagenet and Tudor monarchs. Indeed, no king of the low mental calibre of the Georges ever sat upon the Scottish throne. On this point the old ballad put the feeling of the Scottish people admirably—

> "Wha the deil hae we gotten for a king,
>   But a wee, wee German lairdie!
> When we gaed owre tae bring him hame,
>   He was delvin' in his kail yairdie.
> He was sheughin' kail, and layin' leeks,
> Without the hose, and but the breeks;
> And up his beggar duds he cleeks,
>   This wee, wee German lairdie."

The laws of the Scots kingdom made kingly tyranny difficult, just as the old Scottish pre-feudal laws made difficult the tyranny of the great lords and chiefs. It was the feudal system that made it easy in both countries.

Save in the set-back due to the Norse invasions, Scotland suffered no more terrible calamity than the persecutions of Edward I. and his efforts to convert the country into an English province. The only satisfaction is that they ended in utter failure, and brought the commons into the field, as men whose honour and weal were alike concerned in keeping their country independent. This was a negative kind of benefit, and it is probable that the same end would have been far better served by other and less costly means; but it is a benefit of which historians of a certain type have made much, as they have of the Norse invasions—as though a great war can be a benefit, can be anything other than a great calamity; as though invasions by North American Indians could be anything less than a great curse to a civilised community. What the Norsemen and the feudal system robbed us of was a national culture which had grown up during a thousand years, a culture which was our own, which had received the imprint of our race, and which had splendid prospects of development.

There was little of patriotism in the thirteen candidates who came forward to claim the crown of Alexander III. on his sad and sudden death by the fall of his horse over the cliffs at Kinghorn in Fife. Only two of them, indeed, had any real claim; but it suited Edward's purpose to cause difficulty and confusion, so that in making his award as umpire he might place the successful candidate under an obligation to himself. It cannot be said that the candidates were in any sense Scottish in feeling or sentiment or education; they all had a share of Scottish blood in the female line. It was a dark hour for Scotland this when, as the poet says, her "golde changed into lede." After eighteen months of deliberation, Edward gave his award to John Baliol, a man of weak character but not without courage. As soon as he became king, Edward commenced to heap indignities upon him; assuming the character of an overlord, to which he had no tittle of right, he commanded that any act of injustice, or complaint should be referred to him by the King of Scotland, who must appear before him personally at Westminster. Even Baliol, the "toom tabard," could not stand this kind of degradation, and he threw off his allegiance and invaded England.

Edward had now got what he aimed at, and he marched north with a huge army backed by a great fleet. Taking Berwick, then our first seaport, he slew, in the streets of the town, no less than seventeen thousand persons, and finally utterly routed Baliol's army at Dunbar. He then marched north as far as Elgin, and made himself master of the country. Baliol submitted and did penance before the English knights in the churchyard of Strathcathro. His crown was taken from his brow, and he was publicly unfrocked, while he stood and admitted his guilt, dressed only in his shirt and drawers. The crown he resigned, and he was sent a prisoner to the Tower of London. The insult was deeply felt by the Scottish people. Edward appointed the Earl of Surrey Guardian of Scotland, filled all the castles with English garrisons and the public offices with Englishmen, and took away to Westminster the famous Stone of Destiny on which the Scottish kings had been crowned from immemorial time. It is, however, pretty clear that this "lawyer king," as he has been called, did not remove the national documents as has been stated. Mr. Joseph Bain has cleared this stain from his character. Fearing lest the Scots should join Philip of France in his war against him, he ordered that no

Scotsman should be allowed to leave the kingdom.

This was in January 1296–7. In the winter of the same year a young man, son of Sir Malcolm Wallace of Elderslie in Renfrew, was insulted by the English in the streets of Lanark. With a handful of men and his friend Sir John the Graeme (the remains of whose castle may still be seen near Balfron) they fought their way through the streets to his house, from which they escaped into the woods. The English governor, Haselrig, knowing that Wallace's young sweetheart, the heiress of the Bradfuites of Lamington, had helped their escape, had her put to death; and Wallace, the first of Scottish patriots, who had already been engaged in fighting the invaders, came into prominence by the revenge he exacted for this murder. He broke into the house of the governor, Haselrig, at midnight, and, dragging him into the street, had him instantly beheaded. The people of the town then rose, and slew twelve-score of the men of Edward's garrison.

Some of the nobles now came over to the

popular side. Amongst them, the Steward of Scotland and Sir John Stewart of Bonkill joined Wallace, who united his force, largely composed of Lanark townsmen, with that under Sir William Douglas.

The Stewarts brought into the field the men of Bute and Arran, the famous Brandani; and after the successful campaign in the Glasgow neighbourhood, Wallace appears to have taken them, with "Westland men all sturdy, stout, and bold, five hundred next, Sir John the Graeme he got, Lundie five hundred more," in his march through Glendochart to Brander and Loch Awe to trap the Irish mercenary general, MacFadzean. Thence they seem to have marched to Ardchattan, and here held a kind of conference with the West Highland leaders.

Carrick suggests that it was owing to the growing strength of Wallace's force, and possibly to his severe punishment of deserters of rank, that some of the barons left him a little later.

These deserters included the best of the nobles, like Sir William of Douglas, the

Steward, Stewart of Bonkill, Robert Bruce, Lindsay, and the Bishop of Glasgow, Wishart. Wallace marched north, followed only by his poorer adherents, the free yeomanry of Scotland. These, as Carrick says, were the tenants and descendants of tenants of the crown and church lands, or those who occupied farms on the demesnes of the barons, for which they paid an equivalent rent in money or produce. They had the power "of removing to whatever place they might think most desirable, and owed no military service except to the king for the defence of the country. Among them the independence of Scotland always found its most faithful and stubborn supporters. These *liberi firmarii*, for so they are called in the Chartularies and Chamberlain's Accounts, were considered so useful . . . that, during the minority of the Maid of Norway, a sum of money appears to have been distributed among them as an inducement to remain on the crown lands of Liberton and Lawrencetoun, which they were preparing to leave in consequence of a mortality amongst their cattle."

These and the freemen of the boroughs,

rather than the cottars or villeins who followed the barons, we are told, supplied the material out of which Wallace recruited his ranks; and the extraordinary frequency with which the Scottish nobles, including even the Steward and Robert Bruce himself, changed sides, leaving Wallace for Edward and Edward for Wallace, made little difference beyond disgusting and disheartening the great leader.

At the battle of Stirling Bridge it is probable that Sir John Menteith, on whom the lordship of Arran had been conferred by the Steward, and also Stewart of Bonkill, leader of the Arran men, were all present. The Steward was now on the side of the English, but his tenants were on that of the people. He played a curious part, for, pretending to make peace for the English with the Scots, he turned round upon them when the actual fighting began, and with the Earl of Lennox assisted the Scots in pursuing and killing the English who were trying to save themselves. It may have been a deliberate trick on their part, but it was not an honourable trick. In fact, never did the

CLOUDS MOVING OVER A MOOR
BEN ARDVEN IN DISTANCE
From a painting by
J. LAWTON WINGATE, R.S.A.

great mass of the Scoto-Norman nobility show
in a meaner light than all through this campaign and at the great commoner's battle of
Stirling Bridge, when Wallace unaided, nay,
hindered, by the nobility, utterly annihilated
a huge English army.

THE BRANDANES AT THE BATTLE OF FALKIRK

The most famous achievement of the Brandani was undoubtedly the prolonged resistance
and splendid devotion they showed at the
battle of Falkirk—a battle which, though it
ended in defeat, was one of the things of
which Scotsmen may well be proud. There
Wallace was at his greatest and best, and
there the commoners of Scotland—small lairds,
tacksmen, and "kindly tenants," and the independent clansmen from the non-feudal,
Gaelic-speaking districts of Scotland—showed
best their tenacity and their stern bravery;
for Falkirk, like later Poitiers, was essentially
a soldiers' battle. And of all the soldiers
engaged in it, the name of the "Brandanys"
comes down to us as those who bore the brunt

of the fight. The subsequent references to them in the story of Wallace shows in what high estimation they were held. They it was who withstood and defeated the great attack of Lincoln and Hereford, and the second onslaught by Bek and Bruce, and they it was, "the men who would hazard anything," who at the end of the fight were called upon when Wallace gathered a few chosen men to guard the retreat of the remnant of his army. So effective does their resistance and the generalship of Wallace appear to have been in covering the retreat of his men, that there was no rout or disorder or pursuit; though they were but a handful, the English were glad to allow them to retire unmolested; and it is certain that the Scots were able to bury quietly the dead Sir John the Graeme, and possibly Bonkill, in Falkirk graveyard before their march westwards upon Stirling. It was, indeed, not till four days later that Edward entered that town. He had won, but his army had had their fill of fighting, and he knew it.

The Lord of Arran was at this time, as we have said, Sir John Menteith, who was a

Stewart; Blind Harry tells us how he had joined Wallace:

"Sir John Monteith was then of Arran lord,
To Wallace came and made a plain record,
With witness there by his oath he him band [bound],
Faithful to keep to Wallace and Scotland."

Sir John, "the false Menteith," is one of the most famous figures in Scottish history, as the man who later betrayed Wallace to the English.

The lordship of the island of Arran had been given to him by the Steward of Scotland a very little earlier, but the Arran men followed his nephew Bonkill, brother of the Steward, as the representative of Jane, granddaughter of Angus, son of Somerled.

It is curious that Menteith's brother was at this time governor of the great castle of Rothesay in Edward's interest, while Brodick castle was held by Menteith himself for the Scots. It is clear that the natives were wholly and heartily in sympathy with the popular cause, despite the fact that Rothesay was in the hands of Edward.

The English army which marched on Falkirk, according to English accounts, was a magnificent one : it numbered over 123,000 men, including 3000 horsemen armed at all points, and 4000 hobilers or light horse, while the footmen numbered 80,000 ; but these were not all, for reinforcements came up on the march. The army, moreover, included Edward's splendid veterans who had done such service in the French war. It was supported by a great fleet of vessels anchored in the Forth, with which communication was quite easy by the river Carron, then navigable right up to the present town of Falkirk, Grahamston, and Bainsford—or more properly Briansford ; for the name was taken from that of Brian le Joy, Prior of the Knights Templars in Scotland, who joined Edward and was slain by Wallace's own hand in Callendar Wood, near this spot. With him were many of the Scottish nobles who had also joined Edward, and one of them, the Earl of Angus, who was with Wallace, is said to have sent secret information to Edward as to the position of the Scottish army and of Wallace's intention to make a night attack. So was Scotland betrayed on all sides by her Norman nobility.

On Edward's side were arrayed all the great men of his realm, Lincoln and Hereford, Butler and Clifford, FitzAlan and FitzMarmaduke, Hastings and Bruce.

The Scottish army numbered 30,000, and it had the fatal defect of being almost without cavalry. Wallace was in favour of avoiding so great an army, and adopting a waiting policy by retiring north. There were serious dissensions amongst the three leaders, and much jealousy. So the little army, consisting of spearmen chiefly, paused on that historic plain, close to the remains of the Roman city of Camelon—a plain which had been the battleground of Scotland during so many ages. The three divisions of the army were under Wallace, Comyn, and Sir John Stewart of Bonkill. It is said that Stewart wished to take supreme command, as brother to the High Steward, who was not present; Comyn, again, claimed the command on account of his near kinship to the throne; while Wallace declined to surrender his authority. One remark of Stewart's, quoted by Blind Harry, is of interest, as it shows, whether Stewart actually made it or not, that the retainers of the peers had joined the popular cause independently of their feudal superiors—

> "Then of your men be not so vain, but mind
> Had each his own there would be few left."

" If every nobleman in Scotland were to claim his part of those vassals which now follow your banners, your own personal retainers would make but a sorry appearance in support of your high pretensions." *

Comyn deserted at the beginning of the battle, taking with him 10,000 men; leaving Stewart with his Selkirk archers and his Arran and Bute men, and MacDuff with the men of Fife, to bear the brunt of Hereford's attack. Stewart, according to Blind Harry, met the advancing division of 30,000 men with his 10,000:

> ". . . the brave Stewart stood so fierce and hot,
> That Hareford's men lay dead upon the spot.
> When spears were broke, boldly their swords they drew,
> And many thousand of the Southron slew.
> The rest they fled unto their king with grief,
> Who sent ten thousand for a fresh relief."

* Carrick.

The Brandani fought on though their leader fell early in the day, and Wallace, according to Blind Harry, said—

> "They have done well in that fellon stoure;*
> Rescue them now, and take a high honour."

They had withstood the onset of a whole division, and being freemen, lairds, and free clansmen, and not feudal serfs or vassals, they were used to acting independently, and so, though leaderless, fought on. Wyntoun says:

> "The Scottis thare slayne were in that stoure;
> There Jhon Stwart apon fute,
> Wyth him the Brandanys thare of Bute."

It has been always a sore thing for Scottish historians to believe that Bruce, afterwards the good king, was on Edward's side at that great fight: it is humiliating, but the fact was evidently too universally known during Bruce's own lifetime to be suppressed.

Fordun makes it quite clear, and he wrote about the year 1380, or only some fifty years after the death of Bruce, and must have been born not more than fifteen or twenty years after

* Dust of turmoil.

that event, when the story of the great struggle was in every one's mouth. He says:—

"While the Scots were holding their ground invincible, and could not be broken by either force or stratagem, this Robert of Bruce, with a body of men commanded by Antony de Bek, taking a long circuit round a mountain, attacked the Scots in the rear. Thus the Scots, whose ranks were impenetrable and invincible in front, were cunningly vanquished in the rear." Blind Harry gives the same account.

Wyntoun also, who wrote in 1426, would no doubt have been glad enough to suppress facts which soiled the character of so popular a hero as Bruce, had it been possible to do so. It remained for later historians near to our own day to attempt the task, but, however unpalatable,

"Truth will stand though all things failin'."

Blind Harry tells how the Brandani stood over their fallen leader:

"Sir John the Graym, and mony worthy wicht,
Wepyt in woe for sorrow of that sicht,

When Bruce his battaill apon the Scottis straik,
Thair cruel com* made cowards for to quake;
Lord Cumyn fled to Cummyrnauld away.
About the Scottis the Suthernes lappit they
The men of Bute before thair lord thai stud,
Defendand him, when fell streams of blood,
Were there about in floodis where they went.
Bathed in blood was Bruce's sword and dress,
Through fell slaughter of trewmen of his own.
Soon to the death the Scots were overthrown.

So, exposed to the famous bowmen of England, and surrounded by the men of Bruce and Bek, the close-locked, invincible schiltrons of Brandanes were mown down till they lay heaped up like a wall around their fallen leader. Then Wallace gathered his knights, and, ordering his army to retire towards the Torwood, where they would be protected from Edward's cavalry and bowmen, to cover their retreat—

"He and Sir John the Graham, and Lauder then,
Stayed with three hundred stout West Countrymen,
Expert in war would hazard anything."

So much the great leader thought of our forbears of the West, to whom went the chief honours of that fatal day, though justice has never been done to the fact.

* Arrival.

It was at this time that the good Sir John the Graeme fell, in a conflict, it seems, between the few knights of Wallace's force and those accompanying Bruce's party. The Scottish host, or what was left of it, retired to the Torwood above Larbert on Carron side, and Bruce is described as returning to Edward's tent where he,

"Sitting down in his own vacant seat,
Call'd for no water, but went straight to meat.
Tho' all his weapons and his other weed *
Were stained with blood, yet he began to feed;
The Southron lords did mock him in terms rude,
And said, behold yon Scot eats his own blood!
The king he blenched at this so home a jest,
And caused bring water to the Bruce in haste;
They bade him wash, he told them he would not,
'The blood is mine, which vexes most my thought.'"

HOW THE BRANDANES COVERED THE RETREAT

According to Carrick's account, made up from the English writers, who do not differ materially from the foregoing, the Scottish army, which principally consisted of spearmen or lancers, was arranged in four divisions or

* Clothing and accoutrements.

schiltrons. "Those in the centre held their long spears perpendicular, and stood ready to fill up a vacancy, while each intervening rank gradually sloped their weapons till they came to a level. The front rank kneeling, and the whole closely wedged together, presented to the enemy the appearance of four enormous, impenetrable porcupines, the space between each being filled up with archers." Seeing the strong appearance of the Scots, the king desired to wait, but gave way to the opinions of his followers, and sent forward the Earls of Lincoln and Hereford with a squadron of 30,000 men. Their progress, however, was retarded by an extensive morass, which covered the front of the Scots and obliged their enemies to make a circuit to the west. While thus employed, the powerful squadron under Bishop Bek of Durham managed to get in front of the enemy. Bek, however, on observing the formidable appearance of his opponents, wished to delay the charge till supported by the column under the command of the king. "Stick to thy mass, Bishop," said Ralf Basset of Drayton, "and teach us not what to do in the face of an enemy." "On, then," said Bek; "set on in your own way; we are all soldiers to-day, and bound to do our duty." At this his men rushed forward, and "became engaged with the first schiltron, which was almost simultaneously attacked on the opposite quarter by the division of Lincoln and Hereford which had cleared the morass. The cavalry of the Scots, and a large body of the vassals of John Comyn, immediately wheeled about, and left the field without awaiting the attack. The schiltrons of spearmen, however, stood firm, and repulsed all efforts of their numerous and heavy-armed assailants, who recoiled again and again before the mass of spears. Baffled in their attack, Edward's cavalry charged upon the archers, who, less able to stand their ground against the weight of their mail-clad adversaries, gave way. In the confusion, Sir John Stewart of Bonkill was thrown to the ground, while attempting to rally his followers, the archers of Selkirk, and, though many of them rushed forward to his assistance, their exertions were in vain: their gallant leader fell surrounded by the bodies of his faithful tenantry."

Though heavy squadrons of cavalry were continually pushed forward against the Scottish spearmen, "still they maintained their ranks, and displayed such admirable discipline and stubborn resolution, that Edward, convinced of the inability of breaking their array, suspended the charges of his horsemen, and ordered all his archers and slingers to advance." Of these, it is interesting to note, 40,000 Welsh archers refused to act against the Scots. Langtoft says:

"The Walsch folk that tide did nouther ille nor good;
They held them alle beside, upon a hille they stood.
Where they stood that while, tille the battle was done."

Of the Scottish spearmen he says:

"Ther foremast conrey, their backs together set,
Their speares poynt over poynt, so sare and so thick,
And fast together joined, to see it was ferlike.
As a castle they stood, that were walled with stone,
They wende no man of blood through them should have gone;
These folk was so big, so stalwart and so clean,
Their foyntes forward prikelle, nohut would they wene,
That if all England from Berwick unto Kent,
The therein men fond had been thither sent,

> Stenth should none have had, to perte them through-
> oute,
> So were they set sad with poyntes round about."

The schiltron formation, we are told, was well adapted for defence, and, despite their small number and the vast odds against them, had they been supplied with a good detachment of cavalry to have scattered the terrible archers of Edward, they would have probably held their ground. As it was, they were exposed to clouds of arrows and other missiles till they were reduced, it is estimated, to a fourth of their number, while the chosen English cavalry which had previously tried to move them, sat on their great horses and quietly waited till the cloth yard arrows had done what they, the veterans of the French war, had failed to do. And so the lads of Argyll and Arran and Bute, of Lanark and the Lennox, of Ayr and Renfrew, of Fife and Strathearn and Stirlingshire,—an army which, by the way, would be composed almost entirely of Gaelic-speaking persons,—was gradually mown down till the field was encumbered with their dead, to the number of 15,000 out of an army of 20,000—15,000 of the finest soldiers Europe could then produce.

THE BRANDANES AT PERTH

Sir John the Graeme was buried in the old graveyard of Falkirk, where his grave may still be seen. There the late Marquis of Bute erected a monument to Stewart of Bonkill and the Brandanes, though it is probable that Stewart himself was actually buried in Bute.

After the battle, the leaders had to hide; for Edward's armies went through all the land, and Scotland lay at his feet. For six months she was almost conquered. Bute and Arran were once more regarded as the safe refuges of the patriotic party, and

> "The earl Malcolm and Campbell part, but let
> In Bute, succour with Synclar for to get."

and

> "Adam Wallace, and Lyndsay of Cragye,
> Away they fled by nicht upon the sea;
> And Robert Boid, which was baith wyss and wicht;
> Arane they took to fend them at their micht."

During Wallace's absence in France, the

Scots fought and won the important threefold battle of Roslin, which was then the talk of Europe, and which had given so much encouragement to the Scots. Neither Wallace nor "the Westland men" were present at this battle, of which an excellent account has been written by the late Mr. E. Bruce Low.* In July 1300 Edward again set out to conquer Scotland with a magnificent army; and again in 1302, after a short truce, when Wallace gathered his old friends, Seton, Lauder, and Lundy from the Bass, where they were in hiding, and the Earl of Lennox, Sir Neil Campbell, and the Brandanes from Bute and Arran. For the Brandani had not yet had their fill of fighting, though there was many a sore heart in Arran and Bute, and for many a day Falkirk was remembered by the vacant places it had left.

"The lordis then and good Synclair
Soon out of Bute they made a ballinger †
For good Wallace."

And some time later, when they had no

* In *Chambers's Journal*, 1909.
† A ship or galley.

GREY CLOUDLAND
SOUND OF KILBRANNAN
From a painting by
J. LAWTON WINGATE, R.S.A.

men with which to attack Perth, Wallace says:

> "In to the North therefore let us bound,
> In Ross ye know, good men a strength* have made,
> Here then aff us† they will come without delay;
> Also in Bute the bishop good Sinclair,
> (Fra he get wit he comes without mar)‡
> Good Westland men of Arane and Rauchle,
> If they be warned they will all come to me."

So—

> "Byscop Synclar intill all haste him dycht
> Com out of Bute with seemly men to sicht;
> Out of the isles of Rauchle and Aran."

They appear to have been with Wallace in his adventures till his capture by means of Sir John Stewart of Menteith, but we have no details of their doings. The great patriot was captured on 5th August 1305. Attempts have been made to whitewash Menteith, but the fact remains that he, a friend, a brother in arms, who had been ardently on the side of the people and the independence of Scotland, hunted down and, by a low trick, betrayed the

---

* Castle.   † Let us go.
‡ When he gets knowledge of it he will come without more ado.

patriot who had saved her alike from Edward and from the Scoto-Norman nobles.

EDWARD'S VENGEANCE

According to Hemingford's *Chronicle*, about this time Thomas Bisset of the Glens, in Ireland, lord of the island of Rathlin, which had given so many men to the support of Wallace, and later sheltered Bruce, landed in Arran with a large force, and held it for Edward. Bisset's tenure, however, seems to have been a short one, for in 1306 Sir John Hastings was made Governor of Brodick. In the year previous Wallace had been taken and executed, and Edward also executed an extraordinary number of Bruce's friends, including his brothers Neil, Thomas, and Alexander, his brother-in-law Christopher Seton, and Simon Fraser, the brilliant soldier but extraordinary renegade of Roslin.

PART VIII
HOW THE ARRAN MEN SHELTERED KING ROBERT BRUCE

CHAPTER XIX

THE AMBUSH AT BRODICK CASTLE

MANY romances have left their traces on Arran: that of the dim far-off days of the great monuments of Machrie Moor, the defensive camps, the stone circles; the fine dreamers, thinkers, and artists too, who strove for high ideals in the highly civilised Dalriadic colony, must have left their imprint on Arran more than on any part of Scotland save Kintyre and Knapdale. Finally came the romance of the terrible days of the Norse invasions, days of darkness and of blood; and of the later times when a leader of the island race shattered the power of these arch-enemies of the men of Arran. Yet not one of those stirring stories can compare in picturesqueness, in the immediate touch with our own day, with the charming tale of Bruce's adventures, when, defeated and deserted by all save a mere handful, he sought refuge amongst the bold and faithful hearts of Kintyre and Arran.

It was worthy of the old quixotic spirit of the sons of Somerled, who himself took up the almost hopeless cause of Mac Eth, that Angus and the Islesmen of Arran, who in blood and in spirit traced themselves to the days when King David gave Arran to Somerled, should receive with open arms the deserted King of Scots: that at the moment when most men worshipped the rising sun, they should turn to that which seemed almost submerged in the western waters.

Barbour, in his poem of "The Bruce," tells this, Arran's most moving story :—

> "To King Robert again go we,
> That in Rauchryne with his men,
> Lay till the winter near was gane,
> And of that Ile his met has ta'en.
> James of Douglas was angry
> That they so long should idle lie,
> And to Sir Robert Boyd said he:
> 'The poor folk of this countree
> Are chargit upon great manner
> Of us, that idle lies here.
> And I hear say, that in Arane,

SHELTER OF KING ROBERT BRUCE

In-till a stith castell of stane,
Are English men that, with strong hand,
Holds the lordship of that land.
Go we thither; and well may fall,
Annoy them in some way we sall.'
Sir Robert said, 'I grant thar-till;
To lie here more were little skill:
Therefore to Arane pas will we,
For I know right well that countree,
And the castle also know I. . . .'
With that they buskit them on-aue,
And at the king their leave have ta'en,
And went them forth then on their way.
Into Kintyre soon come are they;
Then rowed always close to land,
Till at the night was near at hand;
Then to Arane they went their way,
And safely there arrivit they.*
And under a brae their galley drew,
And then it holdit well enew
Their tackle, oars, and their stere;
They hide all in the same manere.
And held their way right in the night,
So that, or day was dawned light,
They were ambushed the castle near,
Armit in the best manere;
And though they wet were and wearie,
And for lang fasting all hungry,
They thought to hold them all privie
Till that they well their point might see.
Sir John the Hastings, at that tide
With knights of full mickle pride,
With squires and good yeomanry,
That were a weill great company,

---

* They landed in Lochranza, and marched through Glen Chamadale to Brodick.

> Was in the Castle of Brodwick . . .
> The time that James of Douglas,
> As I am told, ambushed was;
> So happened at that time by chance,
> With victuals and provisions,
> And with clothing and arms,
> The day before, in the evening,
> The under warden arrived was
> With three boats, quite near the place,
> Where that the folk I spoke of before
> Privily ambushed were.
> Soon from the boats the batis saw them gae,
> Of English men, thirty and mae,
> Charged all with sundry things,
> Some bore wine and some arms . . ."

Douglas and his party then burst from their ambush,

> "And slew all they might overtake.
> The cry raised hideously and high,
> From they, that dreading well to die,
> Right as beasts can roar and cry
> They rushit forth to the fighting;
> But when Douglas saw their coming,
> On his men he knew he could rely.
> And went to meet them hastily.
> And when they of the castle saw . . .
> They fled forouten more debate;
> And they them followed to the gate,
> And slew of them, as they in past."

Douglas and his men then took the arms and provisions they had captured, and went their way.

Ten days later, the king, with all the men

who had followed him, set out in thirty-three small galleys, and "arivit in Arane."

> "And syne to the land is gane,
> And we in a toune took shelter;
> And soon speired carefully,
> If any man could tell tithand
> Of any stranger in that land."

A woman tells him of Douglas and his men, who had discomfited the warden.

> "'Dame,' said the king, 'should you me vis
> To that place where their hiding is,
> I will reward you but lesing:
> For they are all of my own dwelling;
> And I right blithely would them see,
> And right so trow I they would me.'"

And so the good woman led him, though, as the islanders were all Gaelic speakers for five hundred years afterwards, it is certain that, if the poet writes truly, the king must have learnt Gaelic in his youth in his mother's land of Galloway or Carrick.

> "They followed her as she them led,
> Till at the last she shewed the stead,
> To the king in a woody glen."

The place is said by tradition to have been the ancient fort called Tornanschian in Glencloy.

The king wound his horn three times, and Douglas knew the sound, and went forth with Sir Robert Boyd.

> "And blithely welcomed them the king,
> That joyfull was of their meeting,
> And kissed them and speired them
> How they had fared in their hunting."

Bruce, according to the tradition, took up his quarters in the caves of Drumadoon, which are associated with his name, but he later set to work to capture Brodick Castle, and there took up his quarters. The spot is shown in the castle where his little party used to sit and chat and so beguile the time, and the king used to tell stories of chivalry to entertain his men; for he was a genial and kindly man was our strong-armed king, and was not of the sort, as he proved later, who forgot or neglected those who helped them.

BRUCE AND THE SPIDER

According to tradition, the cottage in which the defeated and discouraged king watched the spider in its many attempts to weave its web, as described in the well-known ballad, stood on the shore at Whiting Bay, and the wife of the cottage, the story says, told him his fortune, as Barbour describes, and brought him her two sons to aid in the great fight for the throne. The cottage is said to have stood close by the standing-stone which marks the place of his departure for the Carrick coast.

THE RED LIGHT ON TURNBERRY BEACON

It was from the walls of Brodick that he watched for the red light on Turnberry beacon which was to lead him forth to many perilous adventures. For one day the king decided to send a man to his own realm of Carrick—

> "To spy and speir how the kingdom
> Is led, or who is friend or foe,
> And if he sees we land may too,
> On Turnberry's snook * he may
> Make a fire on a certain day,
> As token to us that we may
> There arrive into safety."

The king then sent one Cuthbert, a native of Carrick, who found, however, that few

* A small promontory or head.

spoke well of the Bruce in Carrick, and that the land, both high and low, hill and valley, was occupied by Englishmen,

> "That despised above all thing
> Robert the Bruce, the doughty king."

He saw that in Turnberry Castle was the Lord Percy with three hundred men, so he decided not to light the fire, but to return to his master.

> "The king that into Arane lay,
> When that coming was the day,
> That he gave to his messenger.
> . . . . . .
> After the fire he looked fast,
> And as soon as the noon was past
> He thought that he saw a fire,
> By Turnberry burning weill schyre;
> And to his men he can it show
> Every man thought that he it saw.
> Then with blithe heart the folk began to cry,
> 'Good king, speed you deliuerly,
> So that we soon in the evening
> Arrive, without perceiving.'
> . . . . . .
> Then in short time men might them see
> Shoot all their galleys to the sea."

And as the king was walking up and down on the shore at Whiting Bay, opposite the Castle of Turnberry, while his men were making all ready, his hostess came to him and told him his fortune. She warns him of terrible things that he must go through, but says that no might or strength of hand shall send him forth again out of his land :—

> "Within short time ye shall be king,
> And have the land at your liking,
> And overcome your foemen all."

And then, to show how much she believed her own prophecy, she gave him her two sons to accompany him. The king thanked her, and was comforted, though not quite convinced; for, as the old poet says :—

> "Indeed it is wonderful, perfay,
> How any man through stars may
> Know the things that are to come,
> Determinedly, all or some.
> . . . . . .
> But me think it were great mastery
> For any astrologer to say
> This shall fall here and on this day."

Barbour says when the king left—

> "This was in spring, when winter-tide
> With his blasts, hideous to bide,
> Was overpast, and birdis smale,
> The thristill and the nightingale,
> Began right merrily to sing.
> . . . . . .

> Into that time the noble king,
> With his fleet and a few menyie,
> Three hunder I trow they might well be,
> Was to the sea furth of Arane."

They rowed across without compass, keeping the fire always in view; and there Cuthbert awaited them, full of fear, for the fire, he said, had not been kindled by him, and all the country was full of Bruce's foes. They held counsel, and Edward Bruce, the king's brother, settled matters by refusing to go back.

THE BRANDANES AT BANNOCKBURN

Then Angus rose—"Lead on, brave Bruce,
 The foemen who thy footsteps cross
In silence wrapped shall sleep to-night,
 Or hie them back owre Milton Moss.

Here stand arrayed my Hielan men,
 From yon green islands by Kintyre;
Clan Cholla and the brave Brandanes;
 Cold is their steel—their hearts are fire!

They stand arrayed to win or die;
 As on its prey the grey gled springs
So shall their claymores swiftly strike
 For honour of a race of kings."

They charge! MacDonald and MacCug,
 MacBride, MacKinnon and MacLoy,
Shoulder to shoulder, foot to foot,
 Like some wild torrent mad with joy.

> And who shall stand and stem that flood?
>   Back to the burn the foe they fling;
> Horo! Hera! the day is ours,
>   And Randolph breaks their wav'ring wing.
>
> Then, 'mid the din of splintering lance
>   And crash of axe on iron mail,
> Down all Clan Cholla's kilted ranks
>   The cry arose, "They fail! they fail!"
>   .   .   .   .   .   .
> And thus they shattered Edward's might,
>   That we, their children, should be free,
> To wanton in the wind that sweeps
>   Our islands by the western sea.—M'K. M'B.

Angus appears to have joined Bruce at the Torwood, near Falkirk, and it was there that the king addressed to him the famous words quoted by Sir Walter Scott: "My hope is constant in thee."

Bruce's army at Bannockburn consisted of 30,000 men, according to Barbour, and the king divided them into four "battels," or divisions: Randolph led the vanguard, Sir Edward Bruce the second division, the Steward, then a boy, with Douglas led the third division, and

> "The fourth battel the noble king
>   Took to himself in governing;
> And had intill his company
>   The men of Carrick all halely,
> And of Argyle and of Kentyr,

> And of the Isles, whereof was Sir
> Angus of Isla and Bute, all they.
> He of the plain land had alsua
> Of armyt men a meikle rout."

The description of the battle is well done by Barbour, and full of detail probably taken down from the tongues of people who had actually been in the fight. A touch of humour is given by a wise old knight, Sir Ingraham Umfraville, who fears the men who would fight on foot, and suggests to Edward that he might win the battle by ordering his army to retire behind their pavilions and tents, and so tempt the enemy to leave their strong position. He had evidently had experience of the Scots; he said to the king—

> ["You shall see that they,
> Despite their lords, shall break away
> And scale* them our harness to take.
> And when we see them scaled away,
> Prik we on them hardily."

The men of Randolph and Douglas and Edward Bruce soon got to blows with the enemy, and so eagerly the Scots fought,

> "That they made neither noise nor cry
> But dang on the other at their might."

* Disperse.

WHITING BAY FROM THE
KILDONAN ROAD
From a painting by
J. LAWTON WINGATE, R.S.A.

SHELTER OF KING ROBERT BRUCE

And when Bruce saw all his three divisions doing well, he brought in "the Westland men" with their terrible axes.

> "So great dinging there was of dints
> As weapons upon weapon stints,
> And of spears so great brusting,
> With such throwing and such thrusting,
> Such girning and groaning, and so great
> A noise, as they can other beat
> . . . . . .
> That it was hideous for to hear."

At Bannockburn, in addition to Islesmen and Highlanders under Angus of Isla and Kintyre, Major tells us that in the force under Douglas and Randolph, Bruce put "seven thousand of the Border youth, who from their earliest years had known no occupation than fighting; along with these he joined three thousand Wild Scots, whose arms consisted of a two-edged battle-axe,* equally sharp on both sides; men, these last, who will rush upon the enemy with the fury of a lioness in fear for her cubs." Again he says: "The Wild Scots rushed upon them in their fury

---

* These axes seem to have been different from the usual single-edged Lochaber axe of the West Highlands, if Major is correct.

as wild boars do: hardly would any weapon make stand against their axes, handled as they knew to handle them; all around them was a very shambles of dead men, and when, stung by wounds, they were yet unable by reason of the long staves of the enemy to come to close quarters, they threw off their plaids, and, as their custom was, did not hesitate to offer their naked bellies to the point of the spear. Now in close contact with the foe, no thought is theirs but of the glorious death that awaited them if only they could compass his death too. Once entered in the heat of the conflict, even as one sheep will follow another, so they, and hold cheap their lives. The whole plain is red with blood; from the higher parts to the lower blood flows in streams. In blood the heroes fought, yea knee-deep."

It would have been interesting to know from which part of Scotland the particular men Major refers to came. He probably refers only to the general custom amongst them.

In Bruce's six invasions of England which

followed Bannockburn, it is probable that the Brandanes were present.

Bruce lived for a time in Arran in 1326 with Menteith, who had long since come over to his cause, and the king gave him back his Arran lordship, and also conferred upon him the district of Knapdale.

PART IX

WHAT THE BRANDANES DID FOR THE STEWARTS

CHAPTER XX

WHAT THE BRANDANES DID FOR THE STEWARTS

THE BATTLE OF THE STONES

THE Brandanes followed Robert Bruce to Tarbert, and were with the Steward in his raids into England at Byland and at York, where the English Queen came so near to being captured. They were also with him at the desperate siege of Berwick in 1319; but the greatest of their services to his house was at the "Battle of the Stones."

When Robert Bruce died in 1329, at only fifty years of age, his son David was a boy of only six years, and Scotland was again plunged into trouble by the ambition of Edward III. of England, who at once commenced his grandfather's old tactics, disregarding the treaty of perpetual peace between the two countries which had been signed in 1328. The treaty had been full of promise for little Scotland as a nation, though it meant bad times for Border reiver and Highland cateran, who had enriched themselves so often by the national pastime of a raid into England, during Bruce's reign.

Edward quietly put up Edward Baliol as king, and bribed the easily purchased nobles of Scotland to lend him their aid when he sent Baliol with an army to invade Scotland. Baliol was crowned at Scone, but the Scottish people were roused, and gathering an army they invaded England. At the famous battle of Halidon Hill they got well beaten, for there they forgot "Bruce's Testament," in which he told them always to avoid the tented field, the formal pitched battle, and to adopt always the tactics of what we would to-day call the guerilla chief. At Halidon Hill the Brandanes were almost annihilated.

The King of England then again invaded Scotland on the rejection of Baliol by the Scots, and reached Glasgow with a large army. He sent his fleet into the Firth of

Forth, and made the Earl of Athol Guardian and Governor of the kingdom. Athol then summoned the freeholders of the Stewartlands—that is, in the south, in Renfrew, Ayr, Carrick, Galloway, Selkirk, and so on, and, having made them swear fealty to Baliol, he marched into the Highlands, and "there was no one who durst gainsay him or proclaim himself Bruce's man."

THE STEWARD'S ESCAPE FROM ROTHESAY CASTLE

About the same time the young Robert Stewart, heir to the throne, who was then fifteen years old, was still, for fear of the enemy, lurking in concealment in Rothesay Castle, and was deriving great comfort from, and having frequent conversations with, "two lovers of peace, friends of King David," John MacGilbride, Captain of Bute, and William Heriot, then sojourning in the barony; and they found means to take him over to Dunbarton Castle, bringing with them the charters of Stewartland.

Stewart, finding his position still dangerous, and resenting the conduct of Athol in laying claim to the Stewart patrimony, took action, sent for his friend the Lord of Lochawe, and soon captured Dunoon Castle. Holinshead (1585) thus describes the famous Battle of the Stones, which was one of the greatest of all the services of the Brandani to the house of Stewart.

"Incontinently, therefore, Robert Steward assembled his friends by the help of Dungall Campbell of Lochquhow, and suddenly took the Castell of Dunoon, sleaing all the Englishmen and others who were found therein. . . . The commons of Bute and Arran, glad of this prosperous beginning, assembled together to the number of 400 persons, and set forward, that they might come to support Robert Steward in such his late begun enterprizes: and being incountered by the way by Alane Lile, shiriff of Bute, they laid so lustilie about them, that they slue the shiriffe (taking prisoner John Gilbert, captaine of the Castell of Bute) there in the field, and discomfited all his people, which they did after this manner.

These people of Bute (called the servants of Bawdanus), seeing such sturs to be made by Alan Lile, ran to a heap of stones not far from them, and with great force pelting the sheriffe, they in the end killed him with stones, and put the rest to flight. Divers of them, taken prisoners, were brought away, and presented to Robert Steward."

The *Book of Pluscarden* gives a few further particulars of this interesting fight. It says that when the natives of the county heard that their lord Robert Stewart had thus entered their country, "there flocked to him . . . a people called the Brandans, who came to his assistance of their own accord."

" The sheriff of the county of Bute, Alan Lisle, then tried to hem the Brandans in on all sides in a narrow pass, and commenced to kill them without mercy. They, seeing themselves unarmed and surrounded by armed men, posted themselves in a strong place, and, waiting the attack, commenced to shower stones upon the sheriff and his men, till they had killed Lyle and many others, and the rest of his army took to flight. They then cut the sheriff's head off and presented it to the Stewart, and also took prisoner John Gilbertson, the captain of Bute."

This appears to be the same Gilbertson or MacGilbride who had secretly, with Heriot, rowed the Steward to Dunbarton Castle. He had evidently been made to swear allegiance to Baliol, like many more, against his will. Gilbertson, we are told,* surrendered the Castle of Bute and did homage to the Steward as "his natural lord," which, with his local name, certainly means that he was a native.

From him branches of the MacBride and Bannatyne families claim descent. Thus genial Robert was able to make a stand in the West, and was there joined by many friends, including Thomas Bruce and the men of Kyle.

For this most notable service of the Brandanes, Holinshead adds that Stewart, "in recompense of this service, granted sundrie privileges unto the inhabitants of Bute and Arran : as, among other things, to be free from paying tribute for their corn and grain. Such

---

* *Book of Pluscarden.*

felicities succeeding one another, caused many of the Scots to join themselves with Robert Steward, in hope to recover the realm out of the Englishmen's hands."

Save Halidon Hill, the Scots had been successful in all their raids, and Edward got little from his invasions till at Neville's Cross, where the Brandani were also present, David II., then a youth of eighteen, refusing the advice of experienced men, suffered utter defeat. The Scots army, gathered from Highlands and Lowlands, made a hasty retreat to the fortresses of the Border country, and King David was carried captive into England by one Sir John Copeland, an English knight.

THE KING'S BODYGUARD

Robert II. did not forget the Brandani, and he made them his bodyguard and gave them charters for their lands, one of which, dated in the second year of his reign, is still possessd by the head of the ancient family of MacLoy or MacLouie of Kilmichael and Whitefarland, who took the name of Fullarton probably from the Ayrshire estate of that name.

THE BATTLES OF WILLIAM THE LYON AND THE DISASTER AT PINKIE

The men of the South Isles were probably amongst the Highland Scots and Galloway men who followed William the Lyon in his two attempts to recover Northumberland and Cumberland, which had been won for Scotland by David I. and foolishly made over to Henry, the English king, by treaty of Malcolm the Maiden, a mere boy. William was taken prisoner when jousting with a small party of knights. Immediately the Gaelic people of Scotland, indignant at the encroachments of feudalism and the fondness of the Scottish monarchs for foreign knights and nobles, massacred the Normans and English, and made what Fordun calls "a most woeful and exceeding great persecution of the English, both in Scotia and Galloway." The island of Arran had reverted to the Stewarts, and the sheriffship of Arran and Bute was given by Robert II. to his natural son, the ancestor of the present Sir Hugh Shaw Stewart of Ardgowan and Blackhall. Stewart's second son was keeper of Brodick Castle in 1445–50, and received for the office the sum of £20 anually, with the revenues of some crown lands in the island.

A little later the chiefs of Kintyre and their men paid Arran a number of visits, in which they took away with them many unconsidered trifles, quite in the old spirit of the Gall Gael. The castles of the island, Lochranza, Brodick, and Kildonan were fortified and garrisoned, and a number of galleys were held in readiness by the Arran lairds. In 1455 the famous Donald Balloch sacked and dismantled Brodick, and in 1462 came the invasion of the Earl of Ross and the Lord of the Isles, their object, according to Gregory, being to upset the Scottish monarchy.

The island of Arran was always an important place, the prop of thrones, the refuge of kings, the cradle of fighting men, the prize of the liberator; but of course the seat of government was not entirely situated in Brodick Castle, and it is difficult to see how these gentlemen, with all their expert knowledge of raids and rebellions, could expect to win the Scottish crown by capturing even that mainstay of royalty! Their navy was composed of the enormous number of five hundred galleys belonging to the Lord of the Isles. As Mr. MacArthur puts it with unconscious humour: "Though the expedition failed to disturb the independence of Scotland, it was most disastrous in its results on the islets of the Clyde."

The islanders and west Highlanders generally were present to the number of four thousand at the disastrous battle of Pinkie in 1547. Beague, a Frenchman, who was an eye-witness, says: "The Highlanders, who show courage on all occasions, gave proof of their conduct at this time, for they kept together in one body, and made a very handsome and orderly retreat. They are armed with broadswords, large bows, and targets."

Only the year previous the islands of Bute and Arran had been burnt by the English, assisted by MacNeill of Barra, and at this time the position of the Hamiltons was rendered precarious and unpleasant from

THE APPROACH OF NIGHT: OVER
THE SOUND OF KILBRANNAN
From a painting by
J. LAWTON WINGATE, R.S.A.

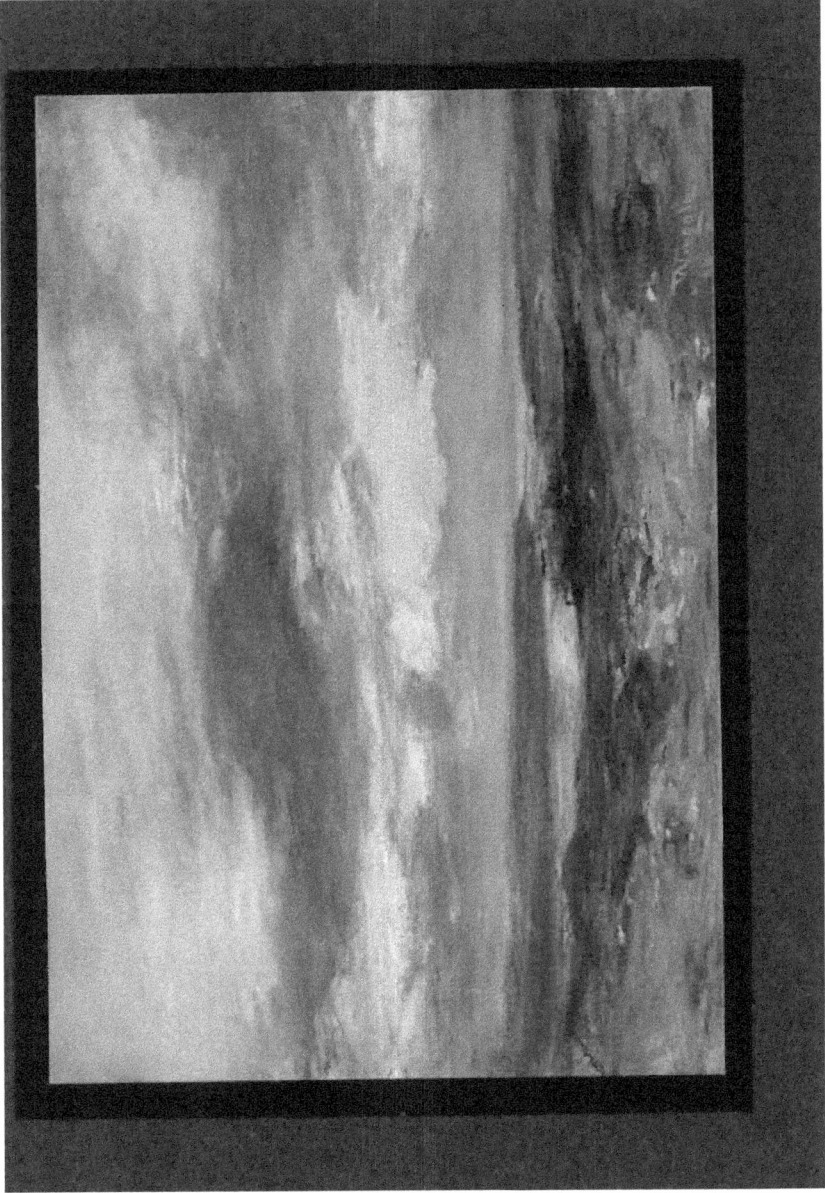

these raids, as is shown by the various bonds they made with the Arran lairds, the MacAllisters, MacCooks, MacDavids, MacBrides, MacKinnons, MacKilgirs, MacCairlies, MacDonalds, and others, for mutual defence in the sixteenth century, not many years after their acquisition of the island.

PART X

THE LATER LORDS OF ARRAN

CHAPTER XXI

THE LATER LORDS OF ARRAN

THE BOYDS

IN 1465 Arran once more changed its rulers, for it was given to the noted Regent, Lord Boyd, the man who had made his fortune by audaciously marrying his son to the Princess Mary, sister of the king. Young Boyd was made Earl of Arran, and received the island as a marriage portion. The Regent became extraordinarily unpopular, being regarded as an upstart by the nobility, and he was ruined and disgraced, so that his son fled, and all his honours were confiscated and bestowed upon the king's eldest son, afterwards James IV.

THE HAMILTONS

The keepership of Brodick Castle and certain farms in Arran were granted to

Hugh, Lord Montgomery, by James IV. in 1488. In 1503 James, Lord Hamilton, husband of the Princess Mary, widow of the Earl of Arran, was made Earl of Arran, and to him were granted the Castle of Brodick and the crown lands of the island. 1506 was the year of the general charter to the crown tenants of Bute, and in this year some of the Kintyre clans, chiefly the MacKays, made a raid upon the island. In 1528 the castle was burnt down by the Argyll clans, but was rebuilt by James V., who was a frequent visitor to the island.

In 1544 Henry VIII. sent a fleet of ships under the Earl of Lennox, which captured and razed to the ground the oft-razed castle of Brodick, and plundered the whole island. Making an Englishman, Sir Rice Mansell, governor, they also took " Rosie " castle, and made the captain prisoner. Brodick was again rebuilt and again raided, and taken by another English expedition, this time under the Earl of Sussex with a party of Irish.

In 1579 the great power of the Hamiltons caused so much jealousy at court that they

THE LATER LORDS OF ARRAN

were deprived of their estates, and Ninian Stewart, nephew of King James VI., was made keeper of Brodick. The title of Earl of Arran was given to James Stewart of Ochiltree, a favourite of the king, who committed so many crimes that the king was ultimately forced to abandon him, and his lordship of Arran reverted to the Hamiltons, in whose hands it has remained since.

"LADY MARY"

The most popular proprietor the island has ever known is undoubtedly the present one, Lady Mary Douglas Hamilton, only child of the twelfth duke. She married the Marquis of Graham in 1906, and she and her husband are much attached to their many-memoried island home. The Grahams from the time of the great and chivalrous Marquis, of Inverlochy fame, always got on well with the Highland folk, and Arran was never so contented or so prosperous as at present.

INDEX

Alexander III., King, at Largs, 149.
  his high qualities as ruler, 160.
Am Bhinnean from the Corrie shore, 6.
Arran, agriculture, state of, in eighteenth century, 54-56.
  Bruce in, 14.
  Burrell's improvements in, 43.
  charm of, 3.
  committee, members of, in 1770, 49.
  Cromwell and, 17.
  ethnology of, 80.
  in the eighteenth century, 40.
  language of, 80.
  mountains of, 5.
  people, condition of, in 1810, 59.
  preachers, famous, 52.
  rent-roll of, in 1778, 61.
  romances of, 12.
  runrig system in, 47.
Athelstan, King, at Brunanburh, 10.

Balfour, J. A., on the word Brandan, 77.
  on St. Brendan's cell, 78.
Balloch, Donald, attacks the isles, 215.
Bannatyne family, descent of, 72.
Barbour's "Brus," 195-197.
Barons of Arran and Bute, 70.
Boyle, Hon. Robert, hides at Auchaleffan, 66.
"Brandane," meaning of the word, *Book of Arran* on, 77.
  Fullarton, on meaning of word, 77.
  Rev. Neil MacBride on meaning of word, 77.
Brandanes, the, at battle of Bannockburn, 198.
  at battle of Falkirk, 169.
  at battle of Halidon Hill, 208.
  at battle of Neville's Cross, 213.
  at battle of Pinkie, 214.
  at "Battle of the Stones," 210.
  at battle of Stirling Bridge, 160.
  at Perth with Wallace, 183.
  follow William the Lyon, 214.

INDEX

Brandanes, the, form the King's bodyguard, 213.
  slay the sheriff of Bute, 210.
  under Wallace, 166.
  what they did for the Stewarts, 207.
Brannan MacLir, 79.
Brendan, St., of Clonfert, 78.
  cell of, in Arran, 78.
  cell of, in Kintyre, 78.
Brian, King, of Munster, his good nature, 13.
Brodick Castle, 189.
  attack on men of, by Douglas, 194.
  captured by Bruce, 194.
Bronze Age burials in Arran, 96.
Brown or MacBraon family, 4.
  Thomas, member of Arran committee of 1770, 48.
Bruce at Bannockburn, 198.
  at Glen Cloy and Drumadoon, 193-194.
  at King's Cross, 194.
  invades England, 292.
  lands in Arran, 193.
  leaves for Turnberry, 195.
  treaty of perpetual peace with England, 208.
Brunanburh, battle of, 126.
Burrell, John, his improvements in Arran, 43.
  his diary, 54.
Bute charter of 1506, 70.

Caisteal Abhail mountain, 5.
Canada, lower, Arran men settle in, 57.
Castle of Arran (Brodick), 27.
Castle of Arran, granted to Montgomery, 29.
  keepers of, 28.
  Lochranza, given by Menteith to Campbell, of Lochawe, 29.
  rebuilding of, 27.
Caves, Bennan Head, ancient remains found at, 33.
  Drumadoon associated with Bruce and with Fion, 31.
  Kilpatrick, the "Preaching Cave," 32.
  Kilpatrick, school held in, 32.
Ceum na Cailleach mountain, 5.
Chaleur Bay, settlement of Arran men at, 7.
Chapels, Arran, 21.
  Kilbride, granted by John of Menteith to monks of Kilwinning, 21, 22.
  Kilbride, removal of ancient sculptured cross from, 23.
  Kilmichael, Glen Cloy, 25.
  Kilmory, 23.
  Kilmory, granted to monks of Kilwinning, 23.
  Kilpatrick, 25.
  Sannox, 26.
  Shisken, 25.
Charters granted to Arran men by Robert II., 73.
Cioch nan h'oige mountain, its changing character, 5.
Cir Mhor mountain, 5.
Clontarf, battle of, 129.
Cook family, see MacCug.
Corrie, 7.
  high, 80.

INDEX

Corrie, Killing Stone at, 18.
Couper, George, member of Arran committee of 1770, 48.
Craig, Peter, his school in the Kilpatrick cave, 32.
Craig na Cuiroch, fort of, 107.
Crawford family, 71, 75.
  now custodians of Baul Muluy, 33.
  Patrick, prize-winner in 1777, 50.
Cromwell and Arran, 17.
  his fear of the Dutch seizing the islands, 17.
  his soldiers killed by the Arran men, 17.
Currie family, 71.
  John, prize-winner in 1776, 50.

Dalriadic colony, its great promise, 13.
Davidson family, see under MacDavid.
Douglas, Sir James, lands in Arran, 191.
  his ambush at Brodick, 192.
Drumadoon, fort at, 104.
  caves at, 31.
Dun Fion, fort at, 106.

Edward I. of England, how he persecuted the Scots, 161.
  his award to Baliol, 163.
  his conduct at Berwick, 164.
Edward III. breaks the treaty of perpetual peace, 208.
Ethnology of Arran, 96.

Evictions in Arran, 57, 58, 59.
  in Highlands, Somerville on, 64.
  in Highlands, MacKenzie on, 64.
  in Highlands, Dr. Donald MacLeod on, 64.

Falkirk, Brandanes at the battle of, 169.
Families, old, in Arran, 69.
  their ancient rights, 46.
Feudal system, evil influence of, 161.
  how it enslaved the people, 162.
Fionn, mythological character, 16.
  his name in word Arran, 16.
  his cave at Drumadoon, 32.
  legends of, in Arran, 16.
Forts and camps, ancient, 104.
Fullarton, see MacLouie, 71, 75.

Gall Gael, meaning of the word, 123.
Geology of Arran, 30.
Glen Ashdale, fort in, 105.
Glen Cloy, Bruce in, 14.
  in Pennant's time, 15.
Glenrickard, meaning of name, 15.
Glen Sannox scenery, 5.
  Chapel, 26.
  hills, 6.
  Killing Stone at, 18.
Goatfell, from Brodick lanes, 7.
  murder of E. R. Rose on, 26.

Godred Crovan, original of Hamlet, 130.
defeated by Somerled, 135.
his tyranny, 134.
the Black King of Man and the Isles, 133.
Gow, David, poem by, 8.

Hakon of Norway at Lamlash, 10.
defeat of, by Alexander, 10.
Hamilton, Duke of, killed at Worcester, 18.
sends letter to Prince Charles Edward, 65.
sympathy with the Stewarts, 65.
Hamilton, Lady Mary, marries the Marquis of Graham, 223.
Hamilton, Lord James, marries the King's sister, 222.
Hamilton, Marquis of loyal to Charles I., 17.
beheaded, 17.
Hamilton, Patrick, member Arran committee, 1770, 48.
John, member Arran committee, 1770, 48.
John, member Arran committee, 1770, 48.
Hamiltons deprived of their titles and estates in 1579, 223.
get grant of Brodick Castle and Crown lands in Arran in 1503, 222.
made Earls of Arran, 222.
restored to their titles, 223.
Harald Harfaager in the Hebrides, 117.

Henderson, Rev. George, on Norse influence on Scotland, 122.
Holy Island, charm of, 10.
cave of Molios and its runic inscription, 11.
Hunter family, 71, 75.

Intermarrying in Arran, statement regarding, 63.
Iona, Christians of, 116.
monastery of, sacked by Norsemen, 123.

Johnson, A. H., on the Northmen, 124.

Kappey, F. E., sonnet on Arran, 1.
Kelso family, 71, 75.
Kennedy family, 71, 75.
Kerr family, 71, 75.
Kilbride graveyard, 22.
ancient cross from, 23.
Kilmichael in Glen Cloy, 15.
Fullartons of, 14.
remains of, at Shisken, 25.

Language of Arran, the importance of preserving it, 81.
Largs, battle of, 143.
Alexander's tactics at, 149.

MacAllister family, 71, 75.
Hector, member of Arran committee of 1770, 48.
John (Rev.), life of, 53.
MacArthur, Rev. John, his book on Arran, 56.
on the old Arran lands, 60.
MacBraon, MacBrayne, or Brown family, 71.

INDEX

MacBride, Neil (Rev.), minister of Kilmory, 53.
   family, 71, 75.
   Neil (Rev.), Lamlash, on the old Arran Barons, 73.
   on the meaning of the word Brandani, 77.
MacBride, Alexander (Rev.), his *New Statistical Account of Kilmory Parish*, 57.
   on the Arran evictions, 57.
   Charles of Shedag and St. Molios Chapel, 23.
   Duncan, member Arran committee of 1770, 48.
   James (writer), on Arran and "the Forty-five," 65.
MacCug or MacCook family of Bennicarigan, 71, 75.
   Archibald, preacher, 53.
   Finlay, preacher, 53.
   John, member of the Arran committee, 1770, 48.
MacDavid or Davidson family, 71, 75.
   Peter, preacher, 53.
MacGregor, Alexander, member of Arran committee of 1770, 48.
   James, sent to Prince Charles Edward with letter by Duke of Hamilton, 65.
   William, 48.
MacKelvie family, 71.
MacKenzie family, 71.
MacKillop family, 71.
   Angus, prize-winner, 1770, 50.
MacKinnon family, 71, 75.

MacKinnon, Alexander, famous preacher, 32.
   Alexander, prize-winner, 1777, 50.
   one of clan killed in encounter with Revenue officers, 32.
MacKintosh family, keepers of Stone Globe of St. Muluy, 35.
MacKirdy family, descent of, 72.
MacLeod, Dr. Donald, on Highland evictions, 64.
MacLouie, MacLoy, or Fullarton of Kilmichael and Whitefarland, family of, 71, 72, 75.
MacMaster family, 71.
MacMhurrich, MacVurich, Murchie, or Currie family, 72.
MacMillan, Angus, preacher, 53.
   Daniel, publisher, 86.
   family, 71.
   of Knap, Argyll, 92.
MacNicol (or Nicol) family, 71.
MacNish family, 71.
Magnus Barefoot in the Hebrides, 130.
   adopts the Highland dress, 132.
   second visit of, 131.
Molios, Saint, Cave of, on Holy Island, 10.
Montgomerys, the, in Arran, 29.
   Alexander, Lochranza Castle granted to, 29.
   of Skelmorlie, Lochranza Castle granted to, 30.

INDEX

Muluy, Saint, virtues of his Stone Globe, 33.
Munro, Neil, his description of Argyll in *John Splendid*, 41.
Murray, Patrick, factor of Arran, 41.

Nicol or MacNicol, Archibald, preacher, 53.
Norman nobility of Scotland, miserable conduct of, 166, 168, 169.
Norse, ancient, type of skull, 100.
    and the feudal system, 115.
    first attacks of, 121.
    in Arran, 114.
    influence on Scotland, 122.
    influence, Rev. George Henderson on, 122.
    influence, A. H. Johnson on, 124.
    type to-day, 101.

Ogg, William, member Arran committee of 1770, 48.

Paterson, John, factor of Arran, on love of country of Arran people, 4.
Pennant on Arran men, 61, 62.
    his description of the songs sung at daily tasks, 62.
    on families who sheltered Bruce, 75.
Pette (?), John, member Arran committee of 1770, 48.
Prehistoric remains in Arran, 91.

Prehistoric remains in Arran, Dr. James Bryce on, 93.
    Dr. T. H. Bryce on, 93, 98.
    The Book of Arran on, 94, 99.

Robertson family, 71.
Rose, Edwin R., murder of, on Goatfell, 26.

Saint Molios' Cell or Kil on Holy Island, 10.
    Bride's, Lochranza, 25.
    Bride's, Lamlash, 22.
    Bride's, Bennan, 25.
    Eoin's Cell, 25.
    Mary's (Kilmory), 23.
    Michael's, Shisken, 25.
    Michael's, Sannox, 26.
    Michael's, Glen Cloy, 25.
    Muluy, his Stone Globe, 33.
    Patrick's Cell, 25.
Scotland, state of agriculture in, 42.
Shaw family, 71.
    Robert, prize-winner, 1777, 50.
    Rev. William, maker of the first Gaelic dictionary, 84.
    his friendship with Dr. Samuel Johnson, 85.
Shisken and Machrie Moor, 118.
Smuggling in Arran, 50.
    in Essex a parallel, 50.
Snorro Sturleson, his account of the battle of Largs, 147.
Somerled, the Hammer of the Norsemen, 137.
    an opposing force to feudalism, 139.

INDEX

Somerled defeats Godred, 142.
  his character, 138.
  his death at Renfrew, 143.
  his great work for Scotland, 137.
  his personal appearance, 139.
  his treaty of 1159, 142.
  marries daughter of King Olave the Red, 136.
Steward Alexander, the, marries Jane, Nic Somerled, 146.
Steward's escape from Rothesay Castle, 209.
Stewart family, 71, 75.
  Rev. Gershom, minister of Kilbride, member of Arran committee, 1770, 48.
  author of the *Old Statistical Account of Kilbride*.
Stewarts, the, as rulers, 160.
Stirling Bridge, battle of, 160.

Stone Age remains in Arran, 92.

Tacitus's description of the Caledonians, 102.
Thomson family, 71.
  Alexander, prize-winner, 1777, 50.
  burial-place at Shisken, 24.
Thorfin, Jarl of Orkney, conquers part of Scotland, 129.
Tornanschian, fort of, described by Pennant, 108.
  Bruce at, 108.

Viking Age in Arran, 114.

Wallace, days of, 159.
  his sweetheart murdered by Haselrig, 165.
White, Captain, on St. Brendan's cell at Skipnish, 78.
Mr. J. A. Balfour on, 78.
Wilson, Sir Daniel, on the Scandinavian type of skull, 100.

Milton Keynes UK
Ingram Content Group UK Ltd.
UKHW041208231023
431175UK00004B/457